MW00424557

Helping Your Anxious Child

"Fight Fears, Overcome Worries, and Cope
with Anxiety in Kids"

KATHERINE GUZMAN

© Copyright 2021 - All rights reserved.

TABLE OF CONTENT

CHAPTER FIVE

CHAPTER SIX

CHAPTER NINE

CHAPTER TEN

CHAPTER ELEVEN

CHAPTER TWELVE

CHAPTER THIRTEEN

CHAPTER FOURTEEN

INTRODUCTION

Finding someone who is absolutely fearless is next to impossible. We all have our fears, worries, and insecurities. It is not just adults; even children harbor all this. Most children are scared of one thing or the other. Some are scared of the dark while others are worried about monsters hiding under the bed. Separation anxiety, excessive fear or worry, panic attacks, social anxiety, and obsessive-compulsive disorder are more common in children than most of us believe. These anxiety-driven conditions can prevent them from leading their life to the fullest and enjoying a happy childhood like they're supposed to.

Unfortunately, the stressful world we live in is becoming increasingly overwhelming for children and adults alike. More and more children these days are incredibly stressed out and exhibiting symptoms of anxiety. Childhood anxiety has become commonplace. Parents and caregivers everywhere worry about what they can do to ease their child's anxiety. Are you wondering what is normal? How can you determine if your child's stress has turned into a severe anxiety disorder? How can you help your child? How can you prevent this anxiety from stressing him out? How can you be a more supportive parent? How do you identify the triggers of anxiety? Are you wondering what causes anxiety? Do you want to help your child break free of this worrying pattern and lead a happy and healthy life? Are all these questions bothering you? If yes, this book is the ideal choice for you. Regardless of how worrying anxiety might seem, it doesn't have to be your child's permanent companion.

There are several things you cannot regulate or control in life. Parenting an anxiety-ridden child might make you feel quite helpless at times. Don't let this worry get the better of you. Even if it seems worrisome, it can be managed. Anxiety can be efficiently managed and overcome. It takes conscious effort, patience, consistency, resilience, and implementation of helpful anxiety-coping techniques. Anxiety can be managed. The first step is to learn more about it. Are you wondering how you can do all this? Well, you no longer have to worry, because *Helping Your Anxious Child: Fight Fears, Overcome Worries and Cope with Anxiety in Kids* has all the information you need. The information given in this book will help reduce and even prevent your child's needless suffering. You can also ensure that he is equipped with all the tools needed to lead a good life tomorrow. As a parent, we all try to create the best possible life for our kids. If you want your child to look forward to a happy and anxiety-free future, this book will come in handy.

In this book, you will learn about understanding fears and anxiety in children, and their common causes and triggers. The first step toward tackling anxiety in your child is to educate yourself about it. Always remember that information is the most powerful tool in your arsenal to tackle anxiety. The more you are aware of anxiety, the easier it is to recognize whether your child is suffering from it or not. You will also be introduced to how anxiety works and the different thought patterns your child might be suffering from. Once you are armed with this information, you will learn to recognize your child's anxiety triggers and his fears or worries. Knowingly or unknowingly, a common mistake most parents (even the well-intentioned ones) make is feeding their child fears. Fear is contagious, and if you are not careful, it can quickly become overwhelming. As a parent, it is your responsibility to stay calm and confident even in stressful circumstances. Remember, your child is depending and counting on you. You need to be his pillar of strength and support during his anxiety.

By understanding the different types of anxiety disorders, the common causes, and how you can help your child cope with them, you can increase his confidence and sense of independence. You should also understand how to stop feeding your child's fears and prevent his fears from feeding his anxiety. When it comes to anxiety, negative thought patterns and behaviors have a direct effect on anxiety. One factor leads to another and it is a vicious cycle. Unless you know what to look for, you cannot help your child overcome anxiety. This is where this book steps into the picture. It will teach you about common myths associated with anxiety, different signs you should watch out for, helping your child understand anxiety, and opening a healthy dialogue about anxiety and mental health. Mental health is as important as physical and emotional health. Even if one of these aspects of your child's life is out of balance, it adversely affects everything else.

Teaching your child to think realistically and providing him with the skills required to face and fight his fears and plan for a brighter future can help him cope with his anxiety. Anxiety is not a condition that goes away overnight. Instead, it takes regular conditioning, healthy changes, and consciously changing thinking and behaviors. It is a lifelong journey. Parenting is a lifelong journey, too, and all the information you need to do all this is given in this book. This book will act as your guide and mentor every step of the way.

Are you wondering how I know all this? Well, I believe a little introduction is needed. My name is Katherine Guzman, and I know what you are experiencing right now. I get how difficult parenting can be at times. It becomes even trickier while dealing with an anxious child. My life is everything I ever hoped for. I have a wonderful husband and a 10-year-old who is the apple of my eye. As a doting mother, I was quite worried when my child started showing symptoms of anxiety. This is when I realized anxiety doesn't just affect adults, but even kids struggle with it. Seeing my little one cling to me at parties instead of mingling with his peers or wake up screaming in the middle of the night used to worry me. My child first started showing signs and symptoms of anxiety about four years ago. I was shocked and alarmed when the pediatrician told me that my son has anxiety!

Instead of getting caught up with all my fears and worries, I decided to embrace this news. Anxiety might sound troubling, but it can be managed. I realized it is not the end of the road. I also realized that my son needed me now more than ever. To deal with his anxiety, I started intensively researching what anxiety means, its causes, common triggers, symptoms, and warning signs, and how to deal with it. I spent countless hours poring over all the books on dealing with anxiety in children. From self-help to psychology and parenting guides, I read everything I could get my hands on. During this journey, I tried different techniques, tips, and strategies to help my child manage and overcome his anxiety. It all started with a simple change in my mindset and attitude about anxiety and mental health. The more I read, the better equipped I was at dealing with it.

I started to see a positive change in how my son dealt with his anxiety. With age, he got better at expressing his emotions, needs, and preferences. We started working as a collective unit to tackle his problem. I began sharing my successful advice with other parents who were in similar situations. This was my aha moment! I realized my personal experiences coupled with all the information I had amassed gave me first-hand experience of how to deal with an anxious child. I decided this information needs to be shared and shouldn't be restricted. Those I shared my tips and suggestions with found it helpful. This was my motivation to write this book. First and foremost, I am a parent concerned about the wellbeing of my child. As a mother, I get how difficult it can be while coping with your little one's anxiety. The good news is, you are not alone.

As you go through the information given in this book, you will understand the different nuances of anxiety and how to deal with it. You will learn about certain dos and don'ts of dealing with your anxious child. You will be introduced to a plethora of techniques that can be effectively taught to your little one to manage his anxiety. You will feel more empowered and confident in your parenting skills and abilities by the end of this book. I will use this book to help parents learn all about anxiety in children, so they can help their children fight their fears, overcome their fears, and cope with their anxiety.

So, are you eager to learn more about all this? If yes, it is the best time to get started.

CHAPTER ONE

Deciphering Childhood Fears And Anxiety

"I am scared of dogs!"

"I don't like meeting new kids."

"Can you check my closet before going to bed?"

"I don't want to be alone at night."

"What if other kids at school don't like me?"

"I can't do this!"

Do these phrases sound familiar to you? If yes, chances are your child is expressing his fears and anxieties through them. The first step to help your child overcome his anxiety is to learn about it.

Difference Between Anxiety and Fears

Understanding the difference between anxiety and fear is important if you want to help your child. These terms are often used synonymously but are extremely different. They also have overlapping symptoms, and depending on the context, your child's emotional experience will differ. The rudimentary difference between fear and anxiety is that fear usually comes from a threat that is known or understood. On the other hand, anxiety comes from a threat that is poorly defined or is unknown or unexpected. The stress response triggered by both fear and anxiety is quite similar. For instance, whenever you are scared or anxious, your heart rate increases, your breathing becomes rapid and shallow, and there is muscle tension. All these symptoms are associated with your fight-or-flight stress response required for survival. Without this essential response, your mind cannot fully perceive and understand the danger signals your body needs to prepare itself to tackle the stressor.

Anxiety is usually described as a feeling of apprehension. It is your response to a threat that is not precisely known or unknown. You might feel this unpleasant response while walking alone on a dark street. It can also be associated with the belief that something bad might happen. If you are walking down an empty street late in the night, the possibility of being harmed can trigger anxiety. It is primarily your mind's interpretation of any possible dangers it senses. Anxiety presents itself with various physical sensations that are incredibly uncomfortable. The most common physical feelings of anxiety are muscle tension, pain, tingling or numbness, hot flashes or cold chills, chest pain, rapid heart rate, shortness of breath, involuntary trembling and shaking, tightness in the body, sleeping difficulties, and digestive troubles.

This brings us to fear. Fear is your body's emotional response when it knows there is a definite threat. Let us go back to the previous example of walking down a dark alley. If an armed assailant startles and points a weapon at you, the danger is present right before you. This danger is not only real, but it is imminent and immediate. This becomes the object of fear in the situation. The focus of the response between fear and anxiety might be different, but it is always interrelated. For instance, anxiety stems from an imagined or perceived danger. Similarly, when scared, we tend to experience all the physical symptoms that were previously discussed.

What Is Normal and When to Worry?

What do the boogeyman in the closet, a spider, and a teacher's rebuke have in common? They are all common fears and anxieties children experience. These are things you don't have to worry much about. It's highly unlikely that your child will agree with you. Fears and worries are common. The only thing that makes a difference is how your child handles them. There are multiple sides to every child's fears. Fears keep us safe to a certain degree. They act as an insurance policy and prevent us from doing things we are not supposed to. Some fears we experience are imbibed into our genetics through evolution. For instance, children and adults continue to fear things that are way outside their experience. Similarly, our brains are hardwired to tell us snakes are dangerous and we should protect ourselves from them. Even though an average individual rarely encounters a venomous snake out in the open, we still believe they are dangerous.

Unfortunately, the trouble starts when these fears and anxieties trigger intense emotional responses to specific events or even things. Some are common while others are worrisome. There are times when you need to worry as a parent and others when you need to let go and believe in your child's development.

For instance, infants and toddlers are scared of separation, changes in the usual environment (such as shifting to a new house), mingling with others, loud noise, sudden movements, and even large objects. During the preschool years, children are usually scared of any noise at night, monsters or ghosts, certain animals such as dogs, and the dark. Some common fears children experience during the school years are injuries and illnesses, doctors, failure, rejection, staying alone at home, natural disasters (such as thunderstorms), snakes, and even spiders. All these fears are not only common but are a rite of passage in childhood. As your child grows, he will slowly overcome these fears. The problem with anxiety is the fear never really goes away and instead, it creates intense emotional feelings and experiences that further worsen the existing fears.

Some degree of anxiety in children is appropriate and not alarming. Your child will have fears that come and go throughout his life. Whenever he encounters a new situation, he will need some time to learn about it. After all, he has just started to learn how the world works and is trying to make sense of it. Once he faces the situation and learns about it, he will get used to it. For instance, a child who has never interacted with a dog might be scared of the animal. After spending some time with a friendly puppy, chances are his fear will change.

As mentioned earlier, anxiety is useful to a certain extent. It helps children and adults alike navigate dangerous situations. For instance, you will feel anxious if you are standing at the edge of a cliff. This natural anxiety and worry keeps us alive. This anxiety is even helpful in social situations. For instance, if someone is being bullied or teased, a child might experience anxiety over such mistreatment. This anxiety can give him the courage required to step up and comfort his friend or even defend him. Unfortunately, society has conditioned us to believe that if a child suffers from anxiety, it is a reflection of poor parenting. As discussed previously, children will feel anxious in certain circumstances, and it is perfectly normal.

This brings us to the next question: when is the anxiety a problem that you need to be worried about? There are two red flags you need to pay extra attention to when it comes to anxiety, and they're extreme distress and avoidance. Here is a scenario that will give you a better understanding of these red flags. Let us assume your child just started school and was incredibly happy during the first couple of days. Later, he started to have meltdowns when he was dropped off at school. In fact, he started crying, throwing tantrums, and gasping for breath on the ride to school. Now, let's consider the situation of a child with sensory processing issues such as autism. If a child is extremely sensitive to loud noises and has a strong dislike for them, any situation where loud noises can be expected will make him extremely anxious and nervous.

In both these scenarios, the child might refuse to go to school, or any other place that triggers his anxiety. Another commonality between these scenarios is the extreme distress they experience. These scenarios are a perfect example of childhood anxiety that parents should be worried about. Anxiety comes in different forms and manifests quite differently. If your child is exhibiting any of the following symptoms, it means his anxiety is not normal.

- He goes to great lengths to avoid specific situations, activities, or people because they make him distressed.

- In any scenario, he constantly worries about everything that can and will go wrong.

- All his fears and worries are effectively interfering with his usual activities and preventing him from performing them.

- Regardless of all the reassurances you give, his distress doesn't go away.

- He struggles to sleep at night or keeps waking up in the middle of the night.

- He also complains about physical symptoms such as stomach pain or headaches that are not due to any other medical conditions.

In all these circumstances, your child is experiencing anxiety. If you notice any of these symptoms, consult your child's healthcare provider immediately.

Chemical Imbalances Results in Anxiety

Different types of chemicals are constantly circulating in your body, such as neurotransmitters, hormones, and enzymes. Increased exposure to stress, lack of sufficient nutrition, injuries, age, and even any illness can create chemical imbalances. Whenever there is any talk about chemical imbalances, it's usually referred to as an imbalance of neurotransmitters in the brain. As the name suggests, neurotransmitters are chemicals responsible for transmitting signals from one neuron (brain cell) to another. They also transmit messages from neurons to muscles and even gland cells.

The pathways of the neural systems at times result in emotional pain such as anxiety due to chemical imbalances. When it comes to anxiety, it's usually a combination of factors that results in this condition. It would be unfair to say genetics are the only factors at play. Even if you have a specific gene that increases your risk of anxiety, it doesn't always have to be the case. If you have a predisposition toward anxiety symptoms, other environmental factors need to be considered as triggers. It's usually an interactive combination of factors at play that triggers anxiety.

The neural pathways and associations are responsible for the neurochemicals transmitting in your body. These neural pathways also determine the strength of the chemicals as they pass through synapses. A synapse is the gap between two neurons in the brain. Your neurochemistry is always determined by neural associations and pathways. Certain hormones are needed to ensure the chemical processes are functioning effectively and efficiently in the brain to maintain your mental and emotional stability. These neurotransmitters help with the production and distribution of serotonin. This hormone is responsible for regulating your mood, cognition, learning, and memory.

A hormonal imbalance reduces the distribution of serotonin, which triggers a chain reaction. The lack of sufficient serotonin increases the risk of anxiety. A primary hormone responsible for anxiety and worry is cortisol. Cortisol is a stress hormone and is a part of your body's fight, flight, or freeze response. This response is embedded into our DNA and is a part of our survival instinct. Usually, as soon as a stressor goes away, the fight-or-flight response goes away, and the cortisol returns to the normal level. When this doesn't happen and there is insufficient serotonin in the body, it increases anxious thoughts and feelings.

CHAPTER TWO

What Causes Anxiety?

Tackling and preventing the manifestation of a problem becomes easier when you are aware of its causes. Anxiety isn't restricted to a single underlying factor. Usually, it is a combination of factors that trigger anxiety and they are as follows.

Genetics Count

If a condition is known as hereditary, it means you either have a high risk of developing it or are born with it. It essentially means the genetic factors or genes were passed onto you through your parents. Genes are a primary part of our DNA. They are present in all the cells in the body. Certain treatments and medicines can also change or activate certain genes. The likelihood of inheriting a disease depends on whether the specific genes are activated or not.

Understanding the link between genetics and anxiety is not a new topic in the scientific community. Decades of research have been directed towards this topic. According to the research undertaken by Deborah J. Morris-Rosendahl (2012), certain chromosomal characteristics are associated with panic disorders and intense fears or phobias. According to the study conducted by Matthew N. Davies et al. (2015), the presence of a specific gene known as RBFOX1 can increase the likelihood of developing a generalized anxiety disorder. In the study, researchers were trying to identify the prevalence of mental illnesses in twins and their genetic makeup. According to another study conducted by Michael G. Gottschalk and Domschke (2016), certain anxiety disorders such as generalized anxiety disorder, panic disorder, and social anxiety disorder are all associated with different genes. Genetic anxiety disorder can be inherited due to its association with different genes, according to a review conducted by Michael G. Gottschalk (2017). From all this research, one thing is certain: genetics play an important role when it comes to anxiety. It's not just environmental factors; even basic biology is at play.

From this research, it is clear that if you have a close relative with anxiety, the risk of developing it is higher. Another conclusion is certain genes increase the risk of developing anxiety. Based on certain environmental triggers, these genes can be turned on or off. Scientists are still trying to understand the specific genes associated with anxiety, and further research is needed until they can come to some conclusion.

If anxiety is hereditary, it doesn't mean everyone in the family will develop it. As mentioned, even environmental factors play a role. If your child faces an extremely stressful situation such as disruption in regular family life or traumatic incident, his risk of developing anxiety increases if he already has the said genes present.

Biological Factors at Play

According to the study conducted by Shao Zheng Qin et al. (2014), certain areas of the brain can also influence the development of anxiety and related problems. The amygdala is known as the brain's fear center. If there are any alterations in the development of this important area of the brain, it increases the risk of developing anxiety-related symptoms. The researchers of the study carefully analyzed 76 children between the age of seven to nine years. It's usually believed that this is the age group during which anxiety-related symptoms and behaviors can first be identified. Parents of these children had to complete various assessments designed for measuring the level of anxiety experienced by the children. These kids also have to undergo a noninvasive MRI (magnetic resonance imaging) scan so the scientist could understand the function and structure of the brain.

During this research, they noticed those with high levels of anxiety had a rather enlarged amygdala. It was not only enlarged, but there was also a rapid increase in the connectivity with other regions of the brain responsible for the perception of emotions, attention, and relation of emotions. These levels were quite high in those with anxiety when compared to those who didn't. Since the amygdala is responsible for fear learning and processing emotions based on information, these alterations in the brain's structure and connectivity resulted in higher levels of anxiety. This study brings research a step closer in the right direction of identifying certain biomarkers associated with an increased risk of anxiety.

Environmental Factors

Apart from the factors mentioned so far, certain environmental factors also play a role in the development of childhood anxiety. Environmental factors refer to the child's usual living environment, relationship with family members or caregivers, and exposure to any traumatic events. Experiencing a traumatic life experience such as dealing with their parents' divorce or even the death of a loved one can be quite overwhelming for a child. It can increase the risk of anxiety.

Similarly, the chance of a child developing anxiety if he doesn't get the required care and support from his primary caregivers is also quite high. If the usual environment at home or school the child is exposed to is incredibly stressful, it increases the risk of anxiety. According to the study conducted by Bethany C. Reeb-Sutherland et al. (2017), environmental factors can increase the risk of anxiety in kids. Though this study was based on animal models, the research suggests exposure to high-quality maternal care early in life reduces the risk of anxiety in offspring.

All these factors are interdependent. Biological factors coupled with genetics and environmental factors significantly increase the risk of developing anxiety and related disorders in kids.

Chapter Three

Understanding the Nuances of

Anxiety

Apart from all the different factors discussed in the previous chapter, certain commonly ignored factors are also associated with anxiety. Some children are naturally outgoing while others lean toward introversion . When compared to extroverts, introverts can seem quite anxious. Understanding these nuances gives you a better insight into your child's anxiety.

Personality vs. Anxiety

Your child might be quiet, reserved, or prefer to hang out only with a couple of friends. If so, he is probably shy or introverted. The world we live in is comfortable for extroverts, but what about introverts? An extrovert is quite comfortable in social settings and thrives in such situations. On the other hand, an introvert struggles and can become distressed too. Wrongly labeling your child's introversion or shyness as anxiety can be problematic. The only way to distinguish between these two is by understanding your child's natural personality and not confusing it with anxiety.

When compared to their talkative, outgoing, and slightly impulsive extrovert counterparts, introverts can seem quiet and reserved. They often listen and observe before acting. So how does a child become an introvert? The answer is quite simple actually—they're born that way. Introversion is a part of your child's temperament and a basic characteristic hardwired into him since birth. Introverts and extroverts are built quite differently. A common mistake parents and adults unknowingly make is they wrongly diagnose their child's shyness as social anxiety disorder. There are overlapping similarities, but they are not the same.

Social anxiety disorder is also wrongly understood as an extreme case of shyness. A lot of people fail to get the help needed for social anxiety disorder because they don't recognize it as a psychiatric condition. According to statistics published by the British Psychological Society (2013), even though this disorder shows symptoms and childhood, only half the adults receive the treatment they need. Understand that introverts and shy kids are not just nervous in certain situations. They have a general phobia of social situations. They are quite terrified of how they will be perceived. Even a small interaction such as eating lunch at the school cafeteria can seem like a scary situation for children with social anxiety disorder. This fear is because they worry they might unknowingly do something offensive or embarrassing and others will judge or reject them. Their social anxiety is deep-seated and it transcends the usual meaning of shyness and introversion.

Try to understand your child's personality before wrongly labeling him. Labels tend to stick. For instance, if you brush away your child's social anxiety disorder or separation anxiety and shyness as introversion, you are denying the help he needs. Be an intuitive parent with an inclination toward positive parenting. Talk to your child about his worries. Do not ignore or avoid them. Instead, get to the root of it. By doing this, you get a better insight into what your child is feeling and experiencing.

Role of Developmental Delays

As the name suggests, developmental delay refers to a child who hasn't acquired the developmental skills expected of him at a given age when compared to his peers of the same age. These delays can occur in cognition, motor function, social and behavioral aspects, and language and speech. Different factors cause such delays. Whether it is a genetic or hereditary condition such as Down's syndrome or a metabolic disorder, developmental delays can be quite stressful for the child. Common factors of developmental delays include trauma to the brain, psychosocial trauma (such as post-traumatic stress disorder), infection, prenatal exposure to toxic substances, and disturbances in his usual environment.

A cognitive delay harms your child's ability to think intellectually, manifests as learning difficulties, and also reduces his general awareness. If a child has any cognitive delays, he might have trouble communicating or playing with others. Motor delays occur when your child is unable to coordinate different muscle groups. Whether they are large muscle groups such as the ones present in limbs or smaller ones in hands, these delays can prevent him from performing simple tasks such as holding onto objects or even brushing his teeth.

Another developmental delay is associated with your child's social, emotional, and behavioral aspects. A neurobehavioral disorder such as attention deficit hyperactivity disorder or autism spectrum disorder can harm his social, emotional, and behavioral growth. Due to these imbalances in the brain's development, his ability to process information or react to different situations is quite different from others his age. It can also harm his ability to learn, communicate efficiently with others, or even interact socially. Children with such delays often struggle with their emotional and social skills. Anything from understanding social cues to carrying on a conversation or even initiating conversations become tricky. They might also struggle with handling their emotions or coping with any changes.

Another common delay associated with your child's development is his speech. Speech delay makes it difficult for a child to understand words or even concepts. Having trouble identifying body parts, colors, and shapes to reduced vocabulary and an inability to communicate properly are all symptoms of a speech delay. When compared with other children of his age, he might not be able to form complex sentences or even understand them. Such children usually are quite slow to talk, cannot create meaningful sentences, and mumble.

Are you wondering why you need to understand developmental delays? Once you understand what they are and the areas where your child struggles, it becomes easier to see how it can cause anxiety. For instance, if your child's motor skills are lagging when compared to his peers, he might be worried about it. If all his friends can play ball games but he is still trying to coordinate his muscles, he will feel left out. This can increase the pressure he's already feeling.

According to a review published by David Beck Schatz et al. (2006), a significant portion of children with ADHD and other behavioral delays usually have an anxiety disorder too. The comorbidity between anxiety and ADHD isn't yet fully understood, but research is going on to understand more about it. The potential causes for both these conditions are quite similar and this can be a possible explanation for their comorbidity. According to the research conducted by Valsamma Eapen (2013), developmental delays can increase the risk of mental health disorders, including anxiety disorders in children. If your child is struggling with any developmental disorders, ensure that you address this condition first. It, in turn, will help reduce his anxiety.

Parental Pressure

Parental pressure is quite real. Even well-intended parents tend to unconsciously engage in pressuring their kids to do better. As parents, the child's wellbeing and success become our priorities. Unfortunately, most parents don't realize there is a fine line to tread between encouraging and supporting the child and forcing them into things they are not yet ready for. In the previous section, you were introduced to the role of developmental delays and anxiety. If your child is struggling with different types of developmental delays, chances are he's already anxious about it. Now, if you force him when he's not yet ready, you are worsening his anxiety.

All parents have incredible expectations for their children. We are introducing our kids to a world driven by hyper-competition and perfectionism. We are placing increasing importance on performance, appearance, and status. All these things are incredibly stressful for your little one. Even if your idea is to help him succeed, it is merely worsening his mental health. This is considered to be one of the reasons why anxiety, anxiety-related disorders, depression, and other mental health problems are gradually increasing in children.

Societies and their unreasonable standards tend to weigh heavily on children. You might believe you know the best for your child. Well, you are not leading his life. Parental pressure is similar to a hurricane that damages everything in its path. Whether it is the pressure on your child to socialize more, participate in activities, or do things that other kids his age are doing, it is bad for him. Instead of shaping him and equipping him with the skills required to become an independent and confident adult, you are worsening the pressure.

The world we live in is competitive enough. Your child doesn't need more pressure from you. For instance, if your child has social anxiety, he might not be comfortable in social settings. Going to birthday parties might be something most children enjoy, but he might not. Instead of forcing him to attend such parties, acknowledge what he's feeling and help him overcome his anxiety. By forcing him, you are making him more anxious. Instead of being a demanding parent, take responsibility for the pressure you have unknowingly or knowingly caused. When left unregulated, this can become a traumatic experience for your little one.

If your child has obsessive-compulsive disorder or post-traumatic stress disorder, chances are an event has left him traumatized. In the aftermath, your child might not even feel like himself. He is dealing with the mental, emotional, and physical effects of anxiety. As a parent, it is your responsibility to help relieve these side effects before alleviating his anxiety. Once his fear is addressed, he will feel better. It, in turn, will increase his willingness to be more participative in different activities will increase. If your child is worried about riding a bike, don't force or scare him into it. It will worsen the trauma he is experiencing. Instead, show him there's nothing to worry about and work with him to let go of that fear. Once the fear goes away, he will be more than willing to ride the bike!

CHAPTER FOUR

How Does Anxiety Work?

Anxiety disorders occur on a spectrum. Depending on the condition and the severity of the problem, the intensity of your child's anxiety will differ. Some conditions have specific reasons, causes, and triggers, while others don't. Understanding the different types of anxiety disorders helps identify what your child might be possibly suffering from.

Types of Anxiety Disorders

You might have fond memories of your childhood. While growing up, did you always think life is easy? Were there any instances that triggered fear and worries? Well, chances are your child experiences some fears and worries too. Childhood can be quite anxious. Children are not only expected to learn new skills, but they need to face challenges, overcome their fears, and learn to navigate a world that doesn't always make proper sense. At times, all the stress, fears, and worries can become too much for their little bodies and minds to handle. The normal comforts you provide might not serve the purpose anymore. In such instances, the child might develop a diagnosable anxiety disorder.

Fortunately, anxiety can be treated and managed. It doesn't have to be a debilitating condition. Before you learn more about helping your child cope with his anxiety, it is important to understand the different types of anxiety disorders. These disorders are as follows.

Generalized Anxiety

Generalized anxiety is characterized as a disorder when you're worried about a variety of topics ranging from finances and natural disasters to relationships and everything else happening in life. There is no specific area of your life responsible for your worries because everything becomes worrisome. These worries can be incredibly difficult to regulate and pop up randomly. Focusing on your usual life can become difficult. Children with generalized anxiety disorder usually experience sleep disturbances, muscle tension, reduction in concentration or difficulty paying attention, increased irritability, and fatigue. Your child could probably be worried about family relationships, his friendships, performance at school, and pretty much anything else happening in his life.

Phobias

Any intense fear triggered by a specific situation, object, or animal is known as a phobia. Some common phobias include the fear of injections, going to the dentist, spiders, heights, or dogs. Phobias are often so extreme that an individual with it goes to great extremes to avoid the object or situation that triggers their fears. At times, they experience extreme distress if they try to face it. Fear turns into a phobia when it lasts for at least six months. Learning to distinguish between an age-appropriate fear and phobia is important. For instance, young ones are usually scared of the dark. If a three-year-old is scared of the dark, it doesn't mean she has a phobia. You will learn more about age-appropriate fears and anxieties in the subsequent chapters.

Panic Disorder

It can be quite heart-wrenching when your little one starts crying uncontrollably or is truly inconsolable. A panic disorder is when he experiences panic attacks that prevent him from leading his life. During a panic attack, your child's breathing becomes rapid; he might experience nausea, blurring of vision, shaking, rapid heartbeat, chest pain, and dizziness. He might also be filled with an overwhelming feeling of doom or that the world isn't real. Some complain about an out-of-the-body feeling and experience too.

These attacks can be triggered by something specific or even random occurrences. A panic attack usually reaches its peak intensity within 15 minutes. If a child has this disorder, he probably avoids all situations that can trigger such an attack. He might also experience a constant worry that he will have a similar attack again. It is always better to seek professional help in such situations because a panic disorder shouldn't be confused with a phobia or social anxiety.

Social Anxiety Disorder

If your child has this disorder, chances are he experiences intense fear whenever interacting with his classmates, friends, or even during playtime. This fear manifests itself quite differently. For instance, he might refuse to speak, cling to adults, start crying, or even throw tantrums. Another common symptom of social anxiety disorder is freezing up in social settings. Chances are he will try his best to avoid all social settings and situations that trigger his fears.

Separation Anxiety Disorder

Some form of separation anxiety is quite common in children when they're growing up with this anxiety-related disorder. This is especially true for those between the ages of one to three years. Try to understand that your child is used to your continued presence as a baby and a toddler. If older children start experiencing intense fear or anxiety when separated from their primary caregivers, it can be a sign of separation anxiety disorder. Those with this disorder are commonly plagued with the worry of being separated from their parents and caregivers. This anxiety is so severe your child might start refusing to go anywhere where you are not there. He might also experience physical symptoms such as nausea, headaches, and tummy aches due to this anxiety. Another common symptom you should watch out for is nightmares.

OCD and PTSD

Post-traumatic stress disorder or PTSD and obsessive-compulsive disorder or OCD were previously grouped with other anxiety disorders. Now, they are classified into their own categories. It's not just adults who can experience this, but even children are susceptible to it. These disorders are relatively rare when compared with other forms of anxiety. PTSD is usually triggered due to exposure to a disturbing event. If your child experiences a disturbing event or any series of events that have resulted in unusual coping mechanisms or behaviors, it can be PTSD. If he starts withdrawing himself, has recurring nightmares about the stressful event, has trouble falling asleep, or becomes increasingly clingy and displays other regressive behaviors such as bed-wetting, it can be PTSD.

On the other hand, obsessive-compulsive disorder is the condition wherein children harbor unwanted fears, feelings, and thoughts. These are known as obsessions because they trigger anxiety. To let go of this anxiety they experience, children develop behaviors known as compulsions or rituals. Obsessions are certain fears and thoughts that kids cannot stop thinking about. Your child might be aware of his thoughts but isn't capable of fully making sense of them. For instance, he might believe that breaking a rule or not listening to his parents can have severely harmful consequences, or doing something brings good or bad luck. It essentially results in a condition where he starts performing certain rituals to ensure that everything is in order, safe, clean, or just right. Whether it is washing and cleaning or repeating a specific word or an action, or redoing the same task, there are several ways OCD manifests itself. It is important to seek professional help to get these conditions diagnosed.

Common Myths About Anxiety

Perhaps the most frustrating aspect of parenting a child with anxiety is all the misinformation available these days. The technological revolution has made the availability of information quite easy. After all, all you need to do is enter a query in a search engine and you have all the information needed. Unfortunately, there's a lot of misinformation available about different topics too. Regardless of whom you meet, whether in a personal or professional capacity, everyone seems to have an opinion about anxiety. Seldom are these opinions backed by genuine facts and science. There are several myths about anxiety, and unless you have the right information, you cannot successfully parent an anxious child. In this section, let's bust some common myths about anxiety and replace them with facts.

Myth #1: Anxiety = Poor Parenting

Your parenting style and child's natural personality tend to influence and shape his behavior. That said, anxiety is not the result of poor parenting. From biological predisposition to the general environment, several factors can trigger anxiety. When it comes to dealing with anxiety, it is okay to become aware of your role in raising an anxious child. However, never make the mistake of equating it with poor parenting. You are not the cause of your child's anxiety. Indulging in self-blame will not help you or your child.

Myth #2: Only Adults Suffer From Anxiety Disorders

One of the most common and perhaps damaging myths of all is the assumption that only adults suffer from anxiety disorders. Several reasons can make an adult anxious, such as financial stress, life changes, relationship troubles, or anything else along these lines. Just because adults deal with different worries doesn't mean children are free from worries and stress. Yes, childhood years are relatively easy when compared to the difficulties of adulthood.

According to the research conducted by R. M. Ghandour et al. (2018), approximately 7% of kids between the ages of three and 17 years are diagnosed with anxiety. It means around 4.4 million children in the US alone suffer from clinically diagnosed anxiety and related disorders. These statistics were published by the Center for Disease Control and Prevention (CDC) and it suggests seven to eight out of 100 children suffer from anxiety. These numbers are representative only of the ones who have been clinically diagnosed. Millions of cases go undiagnosed too.

Myth #3: Anxiety Is Synonymous With Laziness

Never assume that anxiety is synonymous with your child's laziness. They are quite brave and hardworking in trying to overcome that anxiety daily. Waking up every day with a mind full of negative thoughts, unpleasant feelings, and difficult emotions is not easy. It takes a lot of courage to prevent these uncomfortable feelings and emotions from taking over. If your child is dealing with anxiety, chances are he withdraws himself and avoids several situations. He's not doing this out of laziness or weakness. If he is unable to do something, chances are it's because of his anxiety. It is a sign that he needs desperate help and support to get over all of it.

Myth #4: The Child Can Stop Feeling Anxious Whenever He Wants To

If only there was a mental switch that helped switch off negative and troubling thoughts. One misconception you need to let go of is that your child can stop feeling anxious whenever he wants to. If only it was that simple, things would be much easier. If your child knew how to stop feeling anxious, don't you think he would have? After all, anxiety prevents him from leading a normal life like his peers. Once anxiety sets in, all rational thought and logic go out the window. Even if your child's fears are unreasonable and his anxiety is caused by an unlikely event such as permanent separation from parents, he cannot understand this! Telling your child that he just needs to relax or calm down doesn't help. Regardless of how logical and sensible your explanations are, it will not get through to him when he's anxious. So, stop believing that your child can instantly turn off his anxiety.

Myth #5: Anxious Children Are Always Shy

Anxiety is not synonymous with personality. Some children are naturally outgoing while others are shy and introverted. Let go of the misconception that anxious children are always shy. Yes, those with social anxiety might struggle in social settings and socializing in general, but this is only one type of anxiety.

Even if a child with social anxiety wants to interact with others, their anxiety prevents them from doing it. On the other hand, shyness is usually a choice that people make because they are more comfortable away from crowds. If your child decides not to interact with others or spend too much time in social settings, it is his choice. It is not anxiety that is preventing him from interacting with others.

Myth #6: Experiencing Something Bad Results in Anxiety

A common misconception about anxiety is that it occurs only if the child experienced something bad. Yes, this can be a probable cause. Specific events or incidents that are especially traumatizing can result in anxiety. For instance, a child who has a phobia of spiders might have had a scary encounter with a spider at some point. On the other hand, there are certain types of anxiety disorders that occurred out of the blue. For instance, a child suffering from separation anxiety might have never been separated from his loved ones but still experiences it.

As mentioned in the earlier chapters, anxiety is triggered by several factors ranging from genetics to the environment. Understanding more about all this increases your ability to deal with an anxious child.

Myth #7: Anxiety is Not a Real Problem

Whether anxiety is diagnosed or not, it is a very real condition. All the different feelings and thoughts associated with anxiety can be paralyzing. They also create negative behavioral cycles and maladaptive coping mechanisms that further worsen the condition. Since anxiety presents itself as varying mental and physical symptoms, it takes a toll on your child's overall health, behavior, and even happiness. Since anything that induces anxiety is difficult to deal with, children often go to great lengths to avoid such triggers. This might seem like misbehavior. If something takes a toll on your child's happiness and health, it is a real problem that cannot be ignored. If he is experiencing anxiety, don't label him as overdramatic or super sensitive. Anxiety is a problem. The sooner you accept, the easier it will be to help your child gain some sense of control.

Never tell your child that whatever he is experiencing is in his head. Even if anxiety is a mental health problem, its physical manifestation cannot be avoided. If your child is anxious, he might experience inexplicable tummy aches, headaches, and fatigue. He will look to you in that situation for comfort and support.

Myth #8: Anxiety Always Looks the Same

We are all unique and how we experience life differs based on our personalities, experiences, and perceptions. Children are unique too, so any anxiety they experience also differs from one child to another. Some children might express their anxiety by shouting, screaming, getting angry, avoiding certain places, or becoming defensive. On the other hand, some might become extremely clingy, hide, or even retreat into their shells. There are several types of anxiety disorders, and how a child experiences them varies greatly. Some children might also experience physical symptoms of anxiety such as rapid breathing, shakes, and tummy troubles. It's not necessary that anxiety presents itself similarly in all children. This is one of the reasons why parents need to be vigilant when it comes to noticing anxiety and symptoms in their kids.

Chapter Five

What to Do If My Child Has Anxiety?

Now that you are aware of what anxiety means and the different types of anxieties, it is time to determine if your child has anxiety. Don't confuse common childhood fears with an anxiety-related disorder. In this chapter, you will be introduced to different symptoms and manifestations of anxiety to watch out for.

Common Signs of Anxiety

If you are suspicious that your child has anxiety or any other related disorder, you need to be vigilant. It's quite usual for children to feel anxious at times. In the previous sections, you were introduced to different causes of anxiety and the difference between common fears and worry. When it comes to distinguishing between what is normal and what you need to worry about, the line is often blurry. Even if children don't have any anxiety problems, they can display anxious behaviors. For instance, your child may refuse to eat his lunch at school or seem upset for no apparent reason, which would be multiple causes or no cause at all. Anxiety often presents itself as physical, emotional, and behavioral signs and symptoms. Once you go through the information in the section, you will know what to watch out for.

Emotional Signs of Anxiety

- Your child might seem angry or irritable for no apparent reason

- Displays extreme emotional sensitivity

- Frequent crying

- Scared of making even small and common mistakes

- Start worrying about things in the future such as starting high school

- Starts getting uncomfortable or expresses worry when separated from caregivers

- Drop-offs, whether at school, daycare, or even a friend's home, seem scary

- Has recurring nightmares about separation from loved ones

- Constantly worried about losing parents or has nightmares about it

Physical Warning Signs of Anxiety

- Refusal to eat food at school or daycare

- Random stomach aches and headaches for no apparent reason

- Reluctance to use the washroom except the one at home

- Involuntary sweating and shaking under stressful circumstances

- Inexplicably distracted, restless, hyperactive, or fidgety

- Constant tension in muscles and body in general

- Difficulty falling or staying asleep

Behavioral Manifestations of Anxiety

- Constant questions about "what ifs," especially about disasters and other worrying occurrences

- Refusal to go to school

- Refusal to mingle with others, complete silence, or preoccupation when expected to work in groups

- Lack of willingness to take part in group activities

- Prefers to stay on his own

- Looks for constant approval from adults in his life, such as caregivers, parents, and teachers

- Tantrums and meltdowns for apparently small reasons

- Has an "I can't do it" attitude even without trying

If you have any suspicions that your child has anxiety, all the caregivers and adults in his life need to stay vigilant and look for the abovementioned signs. Talk to your child's teachers, family members, or anyone else who is involved in your child's life. Consciously work to track patterns and notice his behavior. Talk to his teacher if they have noticed any behavioral or learning challenges in your child. Apart from it, ensure that you consult his pediatrician or healthcare provider about the same.

Common Treatment Options for Anxiety

Anxiety is a clinically diagnosable disorder. As with any other health condition, unless it is treated and managed properly, it can manifest as chronic anxiety. Now that you are aware of the common signs to watch out for, its causes, and possible factors at play, it is important that your child gets the professional guidance required. He can learn to manage and overcome his anxiety with little external help. In this section, let's look at some common treatment options available to treat anxiety.

Cognitive-Behavioral Therapy

Cognitive behavioral therapy or CBT is one of the most efficient ways to treat anxiety disorders. It teaches your child the skills and techniques required to reduce his anxiety on his own. By learning and identifying negative thought patterns and replacing such thoughts and behaviors with positive ones, managing anxiety becomes easier. CBT will also teach him to distinguish realistic thoughts from unrealistic ones. Most of the anxious thoughts are about something that has not yet happened. If your child learns to differentiate between what is happening and what has not yet happened, he can manage his thoughts. Once he learns to control his thoughts, his ability to manage anxiety will automatically improve. In this, your child needs to work with a therapist and consciously and consistently follow whatever he has learned during the therapy sessions. These skills will stay with your child now and forever. Even though it is usually a short-term treatment option, its benefits are long lasting.

Medication

Prescription medicines are commonly used as a part of anxiety treatment. Medication is used as a complementary treatment option with other forms of therapy to manage and overcome anxiety. This can be a short-term or a long-term treatment option depending on the severity of your child's symptoms and his response to the treatment. While consulting your child's healthcare provider, ensure that you follow the policy of full disclosure about any prescription or over-the-counter medicines your child might be using. The doctor will need all the information about your child's health history, family history of illnesses, and other factors before he can prescribe the required medicines.

The most common drugs prescribed to manage anxiety are known as selective serotonin reuptake inhibitors (SSRIs). These are commonly used to treat anxiety disorders in children and adults. Some of these drugs can be used to treat OCD in children too.

Apart from these two commonly used treatment options, two other forms of therapy can be used. The first one is known as acceptance and commitment therapy or ACT and the second is dialectical behavioral therapy or DBT. ACT teaches your child strategies of acceptance and mindfulness. Mindfulness is the simple act of living in the moment and experiencing everything that happens without any judgment. It teaches him to stay in the moment instead of getting worried about what might happen. Since anxiety often stems from the fear of the unknown, by teaching him to stay in the moment, you reduce the risk of anxiety. Mindfulness and acceptance equip your child with the skills required to manage any unwanted or unpleasant feelings, thoughts, and sensations. Dialectical behavioral therapy is designed to help your child accept responsibility for his problems. By showing him how to deal with conflict instead of transforming them into intense negative emotions, his ability to deal with anxiety will improve.

All children are unique and there is no hard and fast rule that what works for one will work for everyone. Some children might respond better to a specific treatment while others need something else. Apart from these common treatment options, there are certain tips and tactics you can follow, and small changes that you can make to your parenting style that will help your child learn to manage his anxiety. You will learn more about all these in the subsequent chapters.

CHAPTER SIX

Learn And Teach About Anxiety

An important aspect of helping your child tackle anxiety is to talk to him about it. Before you can talk to your child about anxiety, ensure that you have all the information you need. This is a conversation that requires a little preparation. In this chapter, you will learn simple techniques you can use while talking about anxiety. You will also learn about some common mistakes to be avoided while having this discussion.

Talk to Your Child About Anxiety

The importance of mental health is being recognized and accepted slowly by society. Until a couple of years ago, conversations about mental health problems and how to deal with them were taboo. Fortunately, these notions are slowly changing. That said, it is saddening that children and teens often don't understand that they're experiencing anxiety. They might even not recognize the anxiety for what it truly is. Instead, chances are they start believing something is wrong with them. For instance, it's quite easy to fixate on the physical manifestations of anxiety, such as stomach aches or unpredictable mood swings. It wouldn't be surprising if your child starts believing he is weak or going out of control due to anxiety. The problem with these thoughts is they're not only debilitating, they also worsen the anxiety and self-consciousness your child is already experiencing.

As a parent, it is important to start talking to a child about what anxiety feels like. Unless you open a healthy and honest conversation about this topic, don't expect your child to be forthcoming. If you have any preexisting notions that talking about anxiety will worsen his anxiety, time to change this. Usually, fears or problems are worse in our heads than they really are. This is true for not just adults, even kids too. So, stop shying away from the topic of mental health and make it a part of daily conversations. If you talk to your child about anxiety and offer helpful information, it becomes easier for him to understand what he's experiencing, its causes or potential reasons, and what can be done to manage it. In this section, let's look at simple steps to follow while talking about anxiety.

Talking About Fears and Worries

In the earlier chapter, you were introduced to the concept of fears and worries, and the common causes of anxiety. Most anxious thoughts stem from known or unknown fears and worries embedded deep in our psyche. The simplest way to start talking about anxiety is by sharing your worries and fears. Perhaps you can sit with your little one and talk about something you were scared of in your childhood. You can talk about how self-conscious you used to feel while meeting people for the first time. Look for fears or worries that you harbored when you were the same age as your kid. Once you talk about these fears and worries, ask him if he has any of these similar worries of yours.

Another simple way to start a conversation about anxiety is by describing a recent situation where you noticed some signs of anxiety displayed by your child. Perhaps he seemed anxious while visiting a new place, had visitors over to your house, or it was a school-related situation. If you notice that your child is anxious, it is important to talk about it and not brush the topic away. Mental health is as important as your child's physical well being. Ignoring, avoiding, or brushing away these instances can prove detrimental to his overall wellbeing and growth. For instance, if you notice that your child was quiet when you had a visitor over, ask him if he was nervous about having a visitor over. Whenever you talk to your little one about this topic, don't use an accusatory tone. There should be no accusations, blaming, or anything negative associated with this conversation.

If your child starts opening up about his anxieties or worries, offer all the reassurance he needs. Tell him it is okay to have these feelings. Remember, his cues of dealing with his worries and fears will depend on how you deal with them. If he sees you panic, he will panic too. Whatever you do, don't lose your cool and instead, showcase your acceptance of his thoughts.

While doing this, don't tell your child to simply relax or stop worrying. It's quite similar to telling a depressed person to stop being sad and become happy. This is not how mental health works. There is no switch that can be turned on or off. If your child is anxious about something and he constantly hears, "don't worry, it'll be okay," "there is no problem here," or "can you stop worrying?" it will worsen the situation. Showing a little empathy can work wonders at the stage.

Delving Into the World of Anxiety

Now that your child has accepted or has started talking about his worries and fears, it is time to communicate what anxiety means. Before you can talk to him about all this, ensure that you spend sufficient time reading through all the information given in the previous chapters. If you feel it's necessary, consult a professional and prepare yourself for this session. You are talking to an impressionable young adult and you need to have the right information.

"Anxiety is not dangerous." Your child might feel uncomfortable whenever he is anxious. Fortunately, this uncomfortable feeling is not permanent. Since you understand this, talk to your child about the same. Tell him that anxiety is not a dangerous or a life-threatening condition. It is not a problem that needs to be worried about as long as you learn to control it.

"Anxiety is quite normal." The simplest way to make your child feel comfortable talking about anxiety is by stating that it is quite normal. Children are already experiencing a lot of changes in their lives while growing up. If they start feeling abnormal because they are experiencing things others are not, it nearly worsens their stress. If you want your child to get over his anxiety, tell him it is perfectly normal. For instance, you can feel anxious right before an exam or while riding a roller coaster. Depending on your child's approach to problem solving, offer required information. If you believe your kid feels better when he has helpful information and facts, offer the same.

"Anxiety is a natural defense mechanism." An efficient way to normalize anxiety is by explaining how it works. Anxiety is a part of our body's natural defense and adaptive mechanism. Tell your kid that whether it is a wild animal chasing him down the forest floor or while preparing for an important test, we all experience anxiety. Anxiety essentially triggers our fight, flight, or freeze response. As the name suggests, your body starts preparing itself for fleeing the threat, fighting it, or freezing.

If he's still struggling to understand this, ask him how he feels before a very important test, big game, or even a speech. Help him identify how his heart beats faster and the body prepares to fight the danger, run away from it, or wait for it to pass. This response is known as anxious arousal. Tell him that as a species, this natural mechanism is a vital part of our survival process. Whenever we experience any anxiety, we fight, flee, or freeze. Perhaps your child has tried to avoid a situation that makes him anxious by escaping it, or maybe he is used to getting angry and lashing out. Another possible response is he completely freezes, his mind goes blank, and he cannot really think. Ask him if he has ever experienced any of these situations. If he has, it will give him a better sense of what anxiety means and how it works.

"Anxiety is like a smoke alarm." Anxiety becomes problematic when it presents itself despite the absence of danger or threat. If your body is constantly in a state of anxious arousal, it cannot function effectively or optimally. In the previous sections, you were asked to normalize childhood anxiety. Yes, worrying and fears are normal, but these are thoughts that need to be regulated. If your child starts living his life based on these fears and worries, he will never get anything done.

Now, it is time to talk to your child about how anxiety can become problematic. A simple analogy is a smoke alarm response. How does the smoke alarm work? A smoke alarm goes off in case of a fire. If the smoke alarm is too sensitive, it might go off even when there is no fire. For instance, the smoke alarm might start ringing if the toast is burning or the cake you are trying hard to bake has turned to ash. Neither of these situations is life-threatening. Unfortunately, the smoke alarm doesn't understand all of this. By using this analogy, an anxious child's internal smoke alarm is malfunctioning and triggering anxiety despite no obvious smoke. The real problem is one neither of these things works like they are supposed to.

Identifying Anxiety

It is important to help your child recognize his anxiety. Perhaps you can tell him that you will be playing the role of detectives and start an investigation about understanding anxiety. There are three steps you need to follow. The first step is to recognize physical symptoms, the second is recognizing anxious thoughts, and the third is recognizing avoidance. Let us look in detail at all these steps.

It's time to recognize the physical symptoms of anxiety. Perhaps you can start with an outline of the human body and ask your kid to identify where he experiences anxiety. For instance, you can tell him that you experience butterflies in your stomach whenever you are doing something new. Or maybe you experience a lump in your throat before a big presentation at work. Depending on your child's age, you can either ask him to point this out on his body or talk about it.

Depending on your child's age, you need to identify his anxiety. For instance, with a young child, you could ask him to give his anxiety a specific name such as the Worry Monster, Mr. Always Worried, or Ms. Worry. On the other hand, older kids might be better responsive to a music analogy. For instance, anxiety is similar to the volume being turned up until it hits an uncomfortable level. Talking about identifying the physical symptoms of anxiety is important to manage it. If your child is aware of the physical cues it comes with, he can take corrective action before anxiety is triggered.

The next step is to help your child identify anxious thoughts. Identifying such thoughts is seldom pleasant and even adults struggle with it. This might not be an easy process, but you need to help your child identify negative or dangerous self-talk which is resulting in his anxiety. For instance, ask your child what he thinks while trying something new. Ask him what he felt on the first day of school. Give him an example of a situation and make note of his reaction. You can ask him how he would feel if he thinks that the first of a school would be quite easy and pleasant. Similarly, ask him how his first day would be if he thinks that others would not like him.

The final step of this process is to recognize avoidance. Here are some questions you can ask your child.

- If you woke up one morning and realized your anxiety disappeared, what would you do?

- What is the first thing you would do and how would you react?

- Is there any specific way in which your friends, family, or teachers would know that you were not anxious anymore?

After your child has given these answers, encourage him to finish the next two sentences.

- My anxiety is preventing me from...

- When I'm not anxious, I can finally...

After your child has completed these three steps, he will have a better understanding of anxiety. You will also be better equipped to recognize anxiety and deal with any avoidance.

What Not To Do

Parenting is not an easy job and it becomes even more difficult when dealing with a child with an anxiety disorder. The first thing you need to do is normalize anxiety and not make a big deal of it. Try to understand that anxious children are dealing with their worries and need you for support and comfort. Even a well-meaning parent might utter words that, instead of alleviating feelings of anxiety, may worsen it. Since you are not experiencing your child's anxiety, chances are that unknowingly, you might make statements that dismiss his feelings. As adults, we don't enjoy being dismissed or told our feelings are not important or don't matter.

Yes, it can be incredibly difficult to watch your child struggle with anxiety. As a parent, your only role in this process is to help him manage and cope with his feelings while removing any potential triggers. In such situations, you need to stay calm, quiet, and positive. The temptation of trying to fix the anxiety can be quite high. Avoid giving in to the temptation because your child takes his behavioral cues from you. Your response to his anxiety can create maladaptive coping mechanisms.

Here are 10 things you should never say while dealing with an anxious child.

It's Not A Big Deal

Perspectives can be quite deceiving in life. Unless you are experiencing something, you don't understand the true intensity or gravity of the situation. This is one of the reasons why most of us struggle with empathy. Unless we have lived through a situation, we don't know what the other person is experiencing. For an anxious child, his worries are a big deal. These worries prevent him from leading a healthy and happy life. They stop him from interacting with his peers and building lasting relationships; they affect his family relationships and can also reduce his performance at school. All these things are a major part of a child's life. These things are a big deal. Instead of telling your child his anxiety is not a big deal, talk about it. Tell him that you understand he's anxious about something. Perhaps you can try a deep breathing exercise or a calming activity.

Stop Worrying

Regardless of how hard you try, you cannot eliminate your child's anxiety by merely telling him "don't worry" or "stop worrying." If only it was this easy. Understand that your child is already worrying. By making such a statement, you are essentially conveying the message that his worries are unacceptable and unreasonable. Apart from invalidating his worries, you make it seem that what he's feeling is not acceptable. This can further intensify and worsen his anxiety. Instead of a dismissive comment, you could probably ask him, "Why don't you tell me more about what you are feeling?" or "Can you tell me about what is worrying you right now?"

There's Nothing To Be Scared Of

We are all scared of different things in our lives. Whether it is judgment or rejection by our peers, these fears never go away. Most of us are scared of failing. The list of fears is truly endless. Understand that your anxious child is also experiencing all these fears. A quick kiss or a pat on the back doesn't dismiss his anxiety or relieve it. If your child is scared of something, telling him that he shouldn't be scared does not work. The best thing you can do is help ease his fears by starting a healthy and positive conversation about it. Fears lose their power when the person dealing with them starts talking about them. This advice applies to children too. Instead of telling him there is nothing to be afraid of, tell your child that you are there with him and you can both fight the fears together. Tell him it is important to talk about his fears instead of keeping them to himself.

You'll Be Fine

Do you ever feel fine when you're overwhelmed by stress and worries? Fine is probably the last thing you feel in such instances. Now, imagine how your child feels if you tell him that he's fine or that he will be fine while dealing with anxiety. This is not an emotion that usually resonates with an anxious mind. His mind is racing and he is overwrought with worries and feelings he is not fully equipped to deal with; he will not feel anything even remotely resembling fine. Instead of telling him that he's fine or he'll be fine, show you are there for him. It's not just your actions, even the words matter. By telling him that you are there for him and he can depend on you, it will ease anxiety.

I'll Do It For You

All children crave independence. An anxious child is no different. Unfortunately, his anxiety usually gets in the way of his need for independence and the strength required to confront his worries. As a parent, you might feel quite helpless to see your child suffer on his own. You might be tempted to swoop in and fix it for him. If you constantly do things for him, try to fix what he's feeling, or don't let him feel what he wants to, it doesn't teach him healthy coping skills. Instead, it teaches him to become codependent. As a parent, it's your responsibility to equip your child with the required life skills and coping mechanisms to get through his life independently. If your child is struggling with anxiety, here is a simple positive phrase you can use. Tell him, "I know how you are feeling right now, and I get it. But I also know you can get through this. I will always be here to support you." At times, all it takes is a little positive encouragement to keep going.

You Need More Sleep

Have you ever struggled to sleep at night while your mind is racing at 100 miles per hour? Maybe you were anxious about a presentation or an interview at work. Whatever the reason, chances are you've experienced anxious nights. If you have ever felt like this, imagine what your child must be feeling! One of the most difficult parts of dealing with childhood anxiety is the inability to go to sleep at night. A worried mind struggles to slow down at the end of the day and rest. Put yourself in your child's shoes and try to perceive the situation from his view. He is not doing this voluntarily and it is not his fault. He needs you to help him sleep some more. So, if you tell him all he needs some more sleep, you're not being helpful. It's merely counterproductive. Instead, here is another approach you can try. Why don't you tell him that you both can spend some time and use a meditation app before bed to promote overall relaxation and better sleep at night?

Stop Thinking

Anyone who has experienced anxiety would love to break free of it. Anxiety is never pleasant and all it does is worsen and amplify all sorts of negative emotions. Well, your child would love to stop feeling anxious right away. It might sound quite easy because anxiety is thought-based. Unfortunately, regulating your thoughts is not an easy process. Even adults struggle with it. How can you expect your little one to understand how to stop anxious thoughts? A positive way to deal with his anxiety is by encouraging him to talk about his anxious thoughts. Start a conversation about what he's feeling, its reasons, and what he wants to do about it. By making him more engaged in this process, you are easing his anxiety.

Can You Hurry Up?

Anxiety can be debilitating. Regardless of what you choose to believe, when your mind is overwhelmed, you cannot process thoughts effectively or efficiently. Understand your child is feeling the same right now. When it comes to parenting, you need to let go of all notions of perfection. Perfectionism is nothing more than a mirage you are chasing. All it leads to is disappointment and negativity. Avoid getting caught in this trap. Anxious kids can be quite slow and usually move at a snail's pace due to their overwhelmed brains. If you ask him to hurry up or force him into things he is not yet ready to do, it merely increases his guilt. If your child already sees his peers do things he's struggling too, such as interact freely with strangers or make friends, telling him to hurry up increases his guilt. If you don't want your child to feel helpless or guilty, stop telling him to hurry up. Instead, ask him what you could do to help.

It's In Your Head

Yes, anxiety is a mood and brain-related disorder. If you dismiss it and tell him it's all in his head, you are merely shaming him. Instead of helping him tackle the anxiety is experiencing, you are increasing his guilt. A simple phrase you should refrain from uttering is, "It's all in your head." Instead, try a more constructive approach. If you realize your child is anxious, tell him his brain is worrying loud right now. Why don't you both practice a relaxing activity to help calm his brain and reduce worries? Perhaps you can go for a walk or visit the nearby park!

I Don't Understand What You Need

One of the worst things you can tell an already anxious child is that you have no idea what he needs. Parenting an anxious child is seldom easy and it can be incredibly exhausting at times. Regardless of what you do, always keep your calm. Remember, your child is depending on you to stay calm and strong to cope with his anxiety. If you express hopelessness, your child will feel worse. It will also heighten his anxiety. Instead of telling him you have no idea what he needs or what has to be done, it's always better to ask him for suggestions. Why don't you ask your child what he would want you to do or what he needs in a given moment? These simple questions help start a positive conversation about anxiety without any unnecessary judgment or shame.

Coping with anxiety takes plenty of time, effort, and consistency. Your child might not have any intention of asking the same question repeatedly or cling to you in social settings. He might also not want to fall apart at the mall or the grocery store. You might think dealing with an anxious child is difficult. Remember, it is always worse for your child. He's still coming to a grip with all the developments going on in his life. Anxiety is just an ordered form of stress. Apart from seeking professional help, the best you can do is be empathetic and compassionate when your child talks about his worries.

CHAPTER SEAVEN

Helping Kids with Anxiety

A common response that parents and primary caregivers have in the life of an anxious child is to step in to solve all their problems. If your kid has any anxious thoughts and feelings, you will want to step in and get rid of these thoughts and feelings. If possible, you will also try to eliminate all sources of such anxiety. For instance, if your child is extremely scared of dogs, it's a reasonable assumption that you would want to keep him away from the neighbor's dog. You might think you are helping, but all of this is counterproductive.

When you help your child avoid all scary situations, you are fueling his anxiety. Instead of equipping him with the required skills to manage anxiety, you are encouraging him to harbor more fears. Apart from this, you are also depriving him of opportunities to learn important coping skills to manage his anxiety. In this section, let's look at some simple tips you can follow to support your anxious child.

Tips for Dealing With Separation Anxiety

Separation anxiety is quite common in infants, toddlers, and even preschoolers. So by the time your child is three years old, he fully understands the anxiety associated with separation. By now, he also understands the effect of this anxiety on his life. Parents and children alike need to prepare themselves and create a plan of action to tackle separation anxiety. In this section, let's look at some simple tips you can use to help your child manage his separation anxiety.

A Goodbye Ritual

Create a quick goodbye ritual that can be used whenever you need to say bye to your child. Whether you were dropping him off at school, the local park, or even his grandma's house, a quick goodbye ritual helps. Always keep the goodbye ritual short, simple, and sweet. Never leave with any fanfare. The longer you linger, the more difficult the transition gets. Ensure that you consistently practice this goodbye ritual whenever you are separating from your child. In a way, it slowly conditions his mind to get used to the separation.

Always Keep Your Promises

It becomes easier for the child to make it through the separation if you keep your promises. If you tell him you will be back to pick him up at a certain time, ensure that you keep this promise. Never make a promise you cannot keep. Regardless of whether he has separation anxiety or not, don't break your promises. It not only teaches him that promises can be broken, but it can create mistrust too.

Undivided Love and Attention

Children not only love their parents' undivided loving attention but also thrive in it. Whenever you need to separate from your child, ensure that you give him your undivided love and attention for a couple of minutes before saying goodbye. Once you have said goodbye, ensure that you quickly dismiss yourself from the situation regardless of all his cries and pleads for you to stay. At times, dealing with separation anxiety in a child is similar to Ferberizing a baby to sleep.

Learn to Be Specific

Separation anxiety stems from an unknown fear of being permanently separated from parents or caregivers. It can manifest as a fear of parents or caregivers falling ill or dying. Since a child is gripped with crippling worries, it's important to talk to him about it. Whenever you leave your child or drop him off somewhere, reassure him that you will be back at a specific time. For instance, if you are dropping off your child at school, mention that you will be back in the evening to pick him up when school ends. Similarly, if you are going somewhere for a conference, tell him when you will be back. While talking to your little one about time, ensure that he understands what you are saying. For instance, if your child is too young and doesn't understand what 3:00 PM means, you can tell him, "Mommy will be back by the time you wake up from your nap and want to eat a snack."

Practice Some Distance

A simple way to get your child accustomed to being away from you is by creating some distance. Whether it is a sleepover at his grandma or friend's home, do this. Initially, your child might refuse to spend the night away from you. In such an instance, encourage him to spend an hour away. Slowly increase this time to two hours, and so on until he can stay for prolonged periods away from you. The simple technique gives your child a chance to prepare himself for separation without letting the anxiety get the better of him.

As your child grows and you practice these steps, the chances of his separation anxiety occurring will reduce. He will learn to adapt without you. Consulting your child pediatrician might offer help and insight into this problem.

Tips for Dealing With Social Anxiety

Children with social anxiety are scared of making mistakes and have an intense fear of failure. It also prevents them from experimenting and trying new things. Your child might not truly understand his potential or even discover his likes if he doesn't get out of his comfort zone. Social anxiety prevents him from doing this. In this section, let's look at some tips you can use to help your child deal with it.

Engage with and help your child by using the PACE technique. It stands for playfulness, acceptance, curiosity, and empathy. This helps your child let go of some of the anxiety he experiences in a situation. Instead of being serious all the time, try a playful approach while dealing with anxiety. If you are calm and composed, your child will automatically pick on your energy and feel it too. Start accepting your child's feelings and communicate the same to him. This will reduce his worries and ease the fear of being judged. When he knows he will be accepted regardless of whatever happens, he will feel more confident to tackle the situation. Be curious and ask him what he's feeling during a stressful situation. Apart from this, show some empathy. This technique helps you connect with your child.

You must talk to him about social anxiety and what it means. You can use this opportunity to discuss some symptoms of anxiety and teach him self-soothing mechanisms. You will learn more about these techniques in the subsequent chapters. A simple way to start a conversation about social anxiety is by admitting that even you get nervous. Encourage the child to admit when he's nervous about something, and to take the first step despite his nervousness. Ask for his feedback after he has performed the activity he was nervous about.

If you believe any activity or scenario in the future will trigger his anxiety, prepare him for it. When a child has all the information about what to expect, managing his anxiety becomes easier. Instead of springing a random event on him that might trigger his anxiety, talking to him about it is always a better option. Discuss in great detail what will happen, when it will happen, how many people will be there, how he needs to respond, and what he will be doing in the given situation. The more information he has, the lesser is the scope for anxious thoughts creeping in. Anxiety is often triggered by missing pieces of information. By talking about it, you reduce the risk of this happening.

Help your child overcome his social anxiety by concentrating more on the process instead of the progress he makes. Taking part in the process is important. If your child is scared of meeting new people, spending time in public settings, or doing anything because he's worried about being judged, encourage him to do all of this. It doesn't matter whether he succeeds or not. The only thing that matters is he took the first step and made some progress. Whenever he makes some progress, offer positive reinforcement. Never expect perfection in life. Expecting perfection from your child is nothing more than a recipe for disaster for everyone involved. It will also increase the stress he feels in a given situation.

An anxious child's anxiety worsens when a parent constantly hovers around them. Don't be a hovering or a helicopter parent. Instead, take a step back. Learn when you need to stop and when to cut your child some slack. Don't try to swoop in and save the day as soon as you notice any mild distress. Wait until he asks for help. Encourage him to solve his problems before you try to save the day.

Schedule some worry time for your child and teach him coping mechanisms. Some common anxiety-coping mechanisms are deep breathing, progressive relaxation, listening to music, and so on. You will learn more about these topics in the subsequent chapters.

Tips for Dealing With Panic Disorder

Panic attacks occur unexpectedly and they are severe episodes of anxiety. These seemingly random out-of-the-blue attacks without any obvious triggers can be quite frightening for the child. As a parent, you might be quite worried when you see your little one struggling with a panic attack. You can also feel a little helpless because of her. You can help him regulate his anxiety by following the different tips discussed in this section to deal with panic disorder.

Always Stay in Control

Your child will lose complete control of himself during a panic attack. So, it is important that you stay completely in control during this attack. Keep calm, talk to him in a gentle and soothing tone, and reassure him. He'll need time and space to calm down and you need to stay in control of the situation.

Talk About Panic Attacks

Your child might be worried about different things associated with a panic attack. It is quite frightening for him to deal with all of it. From the symptoms to unpleasant thoughts and emotions it triggers, it can be too much to handle. He is probably worried that others might ridicule him. He might be scared of losing complete control of his body and mind during the attack itself. The simplest thing you can do to reduce these worries is to talk more about panic attacks. Explain what panic attacks are, how they occur, and what his body feels like during such an attack. Tell him that these panic attacks are quite common and he shouldn't worry too much about them. Another simple way to dispel his worries is to tell him panic attacks are not forever and they are brief. He needs to know that it is okay for him to panic without worrying about judgment from others.

Practice Breathing Exercises

Now that your child understands what a panic attack is and that there is no shame in experiencing it, the next step is to help him gain some sense of control. The simplest way to do this is by practicing breathing exercises. Breathing exercises help calm his body and mind when he's panicking. A panic attack can make him feel quite busy, light-headed, and induce chest pains too. By regulating his breathing, these physical symptoms will go away. Once the physical symptoms go away and his body is calm, the panic attack will ease. Ask him to close his eyes during a panic attack, and take a deep and slow breath through his nose. Encourage him to hold his breath for a second or two before slowly exhaling through his mouth. Breathing through the nose and exhaling through the mouth reduces the physical symptoms of this attack. You can also teach him some self-soothing techniques discussed in the subsequent chapters.

Overcome Fears

If your child's panic attacks are due to specific objects or situations, facing his fears can reduce the risk of these attacks. For instance, if staying in a closed space is a trigger, gradually expose him to this fear. This means he might be scared of traveling in the car or even sitting in his room. Encourage him to slowly spend more time in the car. Come up with fun games and activities you both can play to ease his worries. Fears are often irrational and encouraging him to face them takes away their power over him. You will learn more about helping your child face and manage his fears in the subsequent chapters.

Shift Your Child's Focus

Your child will have several negative thoughts during a panic attack. By shifting his focus to something else like more encouraging, positive, or happier thoughts, the panic he feels will slowly go away. Whether it is his favorite toy or photograph of happy memory, shifting his brain's focus is important. By asking him to go to his happy place or thinking of a happier time, he can calm his mind.

Challenge the Negative Thoughts

How your child thinks influences the severity of the panic he experiences. If most of his thoughts are beyond his control and are negative, it will be unhelpful. By helping him realize his thoughts are not true or are not supported by facts, these unhelpful thoughts can be changed into something more positive or even realistic. You will learn more about teaching realistic thinking to your child in subsequent chapters. For instance, during a panic attack, he might believe he is having a heart attack, which worsens his panic. By helping him challenge this thought and reminding him that it's not a heart attack, the reality of any panic he feels will reduce.

Keep Reassuring Your Child

Apart from all the different tips discussed in the section, there is another thing you need to do and that is to keep reassuring your child during panic attacks. Tell him this too shall pass and it is not a permanent fixture in his life. Even if it feels as if the panic will never ease, tell him it will go away. This is why you need to stay calm and composed when your child is panicking. Reassure that you are there with him every step of the way and he is not alone.

Tips to Deal With Obsessive-Compulsive Disorder (OCD)

When your child feels distressed, you will want to make him feel better. Unknowingly, you might be reinforcing your child's OCD symptoms by performing a routine he demands, changing your behavior to accommodate his rituals, or offering more reassurance than required. When you do all these things, you are unintentionally reinforcing his OCD. Another unintended consequence of such acts is it teaches your child that it is okay to engage in obsessive or compulsive rituals and thoughts. Here are all the different types you can follow to help your child deal with his OCD.

Start By Setting Limits

Seeing your child in distress is not easy. The failure to set any limits can make it even harder for him to recover from OCD. For instance, if your child insists that you cannot enter his room without washing your hands, don't encourage this behavior. An ideal response is to talk to him about his OCD and tell him that you understand how difficult it is for him. After this, set a firm limit that you will not be washing your hands every time you need to enter his room. He might have an outburst or meltdown when you set these limits. You should expect them initially. After a while, he will also get used to this consistency and his anxiety will reduce. By establishing certain boundaries and following them consistently, you are discouraging his obsessive or compulsive behavior and rituals.

Learn To Be Firm

This tip is in tandem with the previous one. It's not just about setting limits, you need to be quite firm with your child. You need to put your foot down and tell him that you will not be encouraging his OCD. If you set a rule, follow through and set consequences for breaking it. That said, don't hurt or punish him whenever he breaks the rules. For instance, if your child believes he needs to lock the door five times to make sure it is firmly locked, tell him you will be doing it only once. Tell him the door is locked and stick by this. Don't encourage him.

Don't Accommodate OCD

Don't try to accommodate his obsessive or compulsive behaviors and rituals. Accommodating them essentially means you are taking part in his ritual by changing your behaviors. When you do this, it motivates him to stick to his rituals instead of working on changing them. Simple acts of accommodation include excessive reassurance; changing your lifestyle, behavior, and plans because of his OCD; or following his compulsive rituals. For instance, if your child is scared of germs and believes he cannot touch anything until it is cleaned thrice, don't do this. When you start accommodating his compulsions or isolated symptoms of OCD, you are enabling his disorder. Don't strengthen or prolong this disorder and try to avoid it. Do not enable his rational thoughts, and instead, work on discrediting them.

Some Don'ts

Don't try to use logic or reason. It might seem like a rational thing to do. After all, your child's OCD behavior and rituals are not logical. However, understand that you are not trying to reason with your child, but with the OCD in his brain. Similarly, do not offer any reassurance to him and tell him not to worry. Don't tell him everyone is safe and okay or that bad things will not happen. You might temporarily ease his discomfort, but it does not offer long-lasting relief. Unless your child learns to stand up for himself, his OCD will keep recurring. Instead, when he is calm, talk to him about his compulsions and obsessions. Reason with him, and present logic only when he is calm and willing to listen.

Don't tell him to stop his behaviors. This is not something your child invented. OCD is similar to a constant and incessant whispering in his head that tells him to do something. There are a lot of negative thoughts also associated with OCD. So, telling your child to stop his behaviors is not an effective treatment. Do not blame him because he is the victim of this disorder. At the same time, don't punish him for giving in to his compulsions. Instead, explain that all the scary thoughts that he has about doing something specific are because of his OCD. Educating him is a great way to reduce the power of all those bizarre and scary thoughts in his mind. Encourage him to separate himself from his OCD.

Be Encouraging

Encourage your child to slowly postpone and change his rituals. Keep doing this until he stops performing the rituals altogether. You can do this by asking what would happen if he doesn't do something. For instance, if your child believes something bad will happen if he doesn't wash his hands five times, encourage him to wash his hands only thrice. Ask him if something bad happened. When nothing bad happens, ask him to wash his hand only twice. Do this until you are down to washing his hands only once. By encouraging him to break free of his patterns and realizing that nothing bad is going to happen because of it, you are slowly replacing the irrational thought with something realistic.

Consistent Approach

Once you have devised a plan to tackle your child's OCD, ensure all adults and caregivers in his life follow this plan too. There needs to be consistency in practice. Consistency brings a sense of comforting familiarity your child will appreciate. The lack of consistency merely increases confusion and will leave your child bewildered. For instance, if other members in the household accommodate his behaviors while you curtail them, he will not know what's expected of him. It will worsen any stress he experiences and his OCD might worsen. For instance, if your idea is to reduce your child's repetitive behaviors, a simple rule you can use is to repeat the behavior only twice. Once you have said this rule, ensure that all the caregivers in his life follow through. While you do this, you need to talk about the decision and the agreed-upon consequences. If one caregiver is lenient or inconsistent, it will fuel your child's OCD and leave him even more confused than ever.

Our brains are designed to form behavior and habits and stick to them. Whenever you try to change a behavior, it is often replaced by something else. You need to be mindful that your child hasn't shifted from one OCD ritual to another. So, be a vigilant parent and alert all the primary caregivers in his life about the same. A little vigilance goes a long way while helping your child tackle OCD.

Apart from all the different tips discussed in the section, another simple thing you need to remember is to be mindful of your own OCD behaviors. If you are diagnosed with OCD or have mild tendencies that resonate with OCD, seek the help you need. By modeling desirable behavior, the risk of reinforcing your child's OCD reduces. You might need to seek professional help to help your child manage his OCD. If your child is getting treated for it, ensure that you are 100% involved in his treatment.

Tips to Deal With Post-Traumatic Stress Disorder

Post-traumatic stress disorder or PTSD, as the name suggests, is a condition that develops after suffering through a traumatic event. If your child has undergone a traumatic event recently, you need to comfort, support, and reassure him that he's safe. You should also provide him the same to help manage his fears, grief, and recover healthily. In this section, let's look at some simple tips all parents can use to help that kid with PTSD.

The first thing you need to do is ensure that your child feels safe. Whether he is a toddler or a preschooler, going the extra mile to make him feel safe and comfortable is important. Whether it is an extra hug or a reassuring pat on the back, these simple gestures will make him feel more safe and secure. This is quite important, especially after he has witnessed a frightening or disturbing event.

Children, regardless of their age, look to their parents for comfort, support, and reassurance. This is even more important after a traumatic event. So, you need to stay calm and composed. If you have anxiety or worries about something, keep them to yourself for now. Unlike the other anxiety-related disorders, your child will not benefit from knowing that you are anxious too. Amidst all the chaos, he's looking to you for comfort. Whenever your child is around, be mindful of your voice and behavior.

Try to maintain a routine as much as you possibly can. Routines might sound boring, but they are comforting and predictable for a child. When he knows what has to be done and when, it brings with it a sense of security. Routines also reassure your child. Whether it is regular bedtime or mealtime, ensure that you follow this routine.

Yes, it was mentioned that you should not share your anxieties with your child for now, but talking about the event helps. Talk to your child about what happened, how it felt, and reassure him that it is okay. Learning the details of a dramatic event from an adult he trusts can work wonders for his mental health right now. Learn to be honest while having this discussion. Also, be brief and don't go into any worrying details. At the same time, encourage your child to ask more questions about what happened. The more information he has, the better equipped he is to deal with the stressful experiences. Don't leave any unnecessary gaps in his imagination that might conjure wild scenarios. Instead, replace it with realistic thoughts and facts. The information you share needs to be age appropriate and something that your child can handle and manage.

Encourage your child to enjoy himself. Just because he has

suffered a traumatic event doesn't mean he needs to stop enjoying his life. Create a positive environment at home and maintain it. Encourage your child to go out, play, and engage with others of his age, and offer him distractions. This distraction brings with it a sense of normalcy that is desirable for children.

Since your child has recently experienced a traumatic event, it is important to prevent his exposure to further trauma. Whether it is news about a specific incident on the TV, social media, or anywhere else, ensure that his exposure to any disturbing news is limited. Limiting the exposure to news coverage at this stage can be quite good. It helps him understand that the traumatic event was only temporary and not a permanent fixture in his life.

Try to understand that all children are unique and they use different coping mechanisms. If your child wants to spend some more time with his friends or needs some space and time for himself, indulge him. It is okay. You don't know what your child is truly experiencing right now. Another simple technique you can use is to talk to him about his feelings. Reassure him that any anger, mistrust, fear, guilt, or sadness he experiences is normal. Some might cry when they're sad or throw a tantrum when angry. Try to accommodate him without going overboard. If it means letting your child cry once in a while, it is okay. Don't force him to do something he doesn't want to. Don't force him to pretend that everything is okay when he's not feeling fine. Also start to normalize emotions and feelings.

Be a good listener. Don't give in to the temptation of lecturing him about what he's supposed to are not supposed to feel. If the event feels overwhelming to him, he will act out. Don't be angry and instead, try to understand how your child is viewing the situation. Adults don't realize it, but children view the same situation quite differently. By understanding his perspective, you get a better sense of why he is worried. This gives you more information about what you can do to ease his worries.

Don't dismiss his feelings and instead acknowledge them. If your child admits he's worried or concerned about something, don't brush it off and tell him that he shouldn't be. Do not embarrass or criticize him or his feelings and thoughts. Instead, create an open environment in the house so that he knows he can come to you in time of his need. At times, a simple acknowledgment of his worries will reduce and ease his fears.

At times, he might ask questions that you don't know the answers to. There can also be instances when you don't know how to respond. In such situations, understand that it is perfectly all right to say that you don't know. You can always get back to your child later. Instead of giving him a wrong answer or filling his head with misinformation, it's better to take your time and get back to him later.

Apart from all these different tips and techniques, you need to help your child relax. Practicing relaxing activities such as listening to music, impromptu exercise, progressive muscle relaxation, and deep breathing can help. You will learn in detail about all these different relaxation techniques later in this book. For now, understand that you need to set some time aside for teaching and practicing these relaxation techniques to your child.

Chapter eight

Strategies to Support An Anxious Child

As a parent, it is your natural tendency to go into a protective mode when your child's anxiety is heightened. You might try to solve his problems or help him in any way to avoid all triggers of anxiety. Chances are you have tried to engineer a lifestyle that's worry-free for him. You are doing all this to help your child avoid his anxiety. Regardless of how well-meaning your intentions are, all this is counterproductive. The best way to teach a child to manage and overcome his anxiety is by equipping him with the required skills and tools to do this. Instead of solving his problems or helping him avoid anxiety, teach him to manage them. After all, the hard truth of life that all parents need to accept at one point or another is that they cannot protect their child all the time. In this section, let's look at some simple and practical strategies you can use to support your child.

Start With Clear Expectations
The sooner you normalize anxiety, the better it is for your child's wellbeing. Stop treating his anxiety like a disability. Don't offer any unnecessary special considerations. Ensure that the expectations for an anxious child are similar to those of a non-anxious child. At the same time, you should also make certain allowances and accommodations to proceed slowly. For instance, children might be quite excited at the prospect of attending parties and spending a lot of time with peers. If your anxious child wants some quiet time to himself and wants to get away from crowds, let him do that. Never force your child to do things he is not yet ready to. It is good to be encouraging and supportive, but there is a fine line between supportive and pushing. Instead of overwhelming a child, concentrate on taking small steps.

By establishing clear expectations, it helps create appropriate benchmarks for your child to reach such expectations. This will give him a chance to finally work through his anxious feelings without getting overwhelmed. It also teaches him to manage anxiety.

Don't Avoid
Whatever you do, avoid avoidance at all costs. Avoiding your child's anxiety triggers will not do anyone any favors. You might think you're protecting him, but you are merely raising a child who is poorly equipped to deal with anxiety. Remember, anxiety will not go away until he learns to manage it. If you are failing to teach him how to manage it, sooner or later he'll get overwhelmed. For instance, if your child experiences anxiety whenever he sees a dog, the solution is not to avoid all dogs. If avoiding all dogs is the solution, it merely validates his anxious thoughts. It might wrongly convey the message to your child that

all dogs are dangerous animals and should be avoided at all costs. Refrain from engaging in behaviors that further strengthen his anxious thoughts. Instead, work on desensitizing him. To desensitize his anxiety triggers, you need to take small steps.

Let us go back to the previous example of anxiety around dogs. If that's the case, you can start with a virtual environment where your child gets a chance to desensitize his fears. Perhaps you can sit together and look at different breeds of dogs online. You might also consider watching some funny or cute videos to make your child more comfortable. While you are doing this, ensure that you are talking about his anxiety and its triggers. Once he is comfortable doing these things, you could take him to the local dog park, stand at a distance, and let him observe dogs while they play. The final step is to encourage him to meet a friendly dog.

Tackling anxiety is not something that can be achieved overnight. Instead, it is a collection of small steps taken over a prolonged period. Always look at the bigger picture while helping your child manage his anxiety. He can learn a lot from his worries and fears. During the stage, your only role is to act as a guide and mentor. Apart from this, give him the support and encouragement required to take these small steps.

Worrying is Not Bad

It was previously mentioned that you should never tell an anxious child to stop worrying. You're also given suggestions about what you can say instead. No one, regardless of whether they're an adult or child, has ever stopped worrying because someone else told them to. When it comes to worries, it is always a personal decision whether you want to indulge it or not. If your child is worrying about something, don't brush his worries aside, ridicule them, or tell them they are meaningless or irrelevant. Instead, set some time aside for him to worry. Give him some worry time daily. Tell him he's free to worry for 20 minutes daily and that's it. During these 20 minutes, sit with him, make a list of his worries, the reasons, and how these worries make him feel. A great way to elevate anxiety is by talking about it. Give him some uninterrupted time to vent his worries without any judgment. While your child is talking, don't interrupt and instead play the role of a good listener. After this, you can sit together and brainstorm some solutions.

Anxiety Coping Kit

Equipping your child with a variety of coping mechanisms and skills is the best way to empower him to control his worries. An efficient technique is to create a list of strategies you can use whenever anxiety strikes. Spend some time, brainstorm simple ideas, and make a note of them. Encourage him to carry this note with him wherever he goes. Alternatively, you can help him memorize the list. Some simple activities you can include in his anxiety coping kit are progressive muscle relaxation, writing about his worries, taking a couple of deep breaths, using a stress ball, talking about his worries, and reframing his thoughts. Encourage him to get help from an adult if his anxiety becomes too much.

Reframing Anxious Thoughts

The thought cycle of anxiety is overwhelming. Whether you are a child or an adult, it never stops being overwhelming. Anxiety increases the feeling of helplessness. Your child unknowingly gets caught in the trap of pondering about all the "what ifs" and "I cant's" as soon as his anxiety spikes. Anxiety-ridden children usually have a black-or-white, all-or-nothing attitude. They are adept at overgeneralizing. This is incredibly problematic. Life cannot be classified as either black or white. For an anxious mind, there are always opposites that exist. For instance, an anxious mind might assume that someone was laughing at them instead of a situation. This worsens the anxiety he might already be experiencing.

A simple yet effective way to strengthen your child's thinking, increase realistic thought patterns, and reduce negativity is by practicing reframing anxious thoughts. Yes, anxious thoughts can be efficiently reframed. After all, they are triggered by uncomfortable thoughts, feelings, and emotions. To do this, set some time aside daily and work on positive reframing with your child. It might not be easy during the initial stages, but it is effective.

For positive reframing, here are some simple questions you can ask your child.

- Is there anything that you are worried about right now?

- What does this worry make you feel?

- What does this specific worry tell you?

- Do you think this worry is genuine? Why don't we see whether it is right or wrong?

- How can we change this thought into something more positive?

As human beings, we all live in groups and crave our peers' approval. It increases the sense of belonging and togetherness. A common fear anxious children have is the fear of being disliked or excluded. If your child is expressing this worry, it is time to help reframe this worry positively. Ask him why he believes this. Perhaps there was some incident at school which formed this thought. Let's assume that your child didn't know the answer to a question when he was asked. As he was fumbling for words, another kid laughed at him. Remember, you are dealing with children here. Your child's peers don't yet have emotional intelligence. After such an incident, your child might be harboring the anxiety that he's disliked at school. Now that you know what his worry is, how it makes him feel, and how it cropped up, it's time to break down the reality of the situation.

Ask him about his usual participation in the class. Ask him about his favorite parts of school activities. Ask him more questions to understand your child's life at school. After this, help reframe his anxious thoughts into something more positive. Help him reframe the situation as follows. "I was hurt when the other kid laughed at me, but it doesn't mean I don't have any other friends at school." Or "I know I felt bad when the kid laughed at me, but there are several other things I enjoy at school." This simple exercise is all about reframing his thoughts and ideas for the better. Instead of fixating on the negative experience, you are helping him concentrate on something more positive. Focusing on the positive helps reduce the power of a negative or anxious thought.

Practice a Little Empathy

Anxiety can be frightening and paralyzing to a certain extent for children. When a child is overwhelmed by his anxious thoughts, performing everyday actions like attending school, mingling with his peers, or playing a sport can also become difficult. It's not uncommon for anxious children to avoid activities that promote uncomfortable thoughts and feelings. They start withdrawing, and when this happens, their discomfort further heightens. Why does this happen? It's because they are seeing their peers do things they are struggling with. It can make them feel like an outsider.

If you notice your child is avoiding fun activities because he's worried about his anxiety, it's time to step in. No, it doesn't mean you push and force him to do things that trigger his anxiety. Instead, it means you become more empathizing and encouraging. By telling him that he is not alone and you understand what he's feeling, the feeling of alienation he might be experiencing will reduce. Normalizing his anxiety will make him feel better. Repeatedly remind him that he is not alone and that you are there with him. If he seems worried about attending a party, instead of forcing him to go, offer some helpful alternatives. For instance, you can tell him, "Why don't you go for an hour and see if you like it?" or "It might be fun to step outside for a while and play with your friends!" You can also tell him, "Mommy will come and get you if you get uncomfortable," or "This is the perfect time to practice anxiety-coping mechanisms we were talking about."

Concentrate on the Basics

Concentrating on your child's basic health is important. If he's physically fit and healthy, his ability to regulate anxiety increases. He doesn't have to attend all parties or play every sport at school.

He does need to slow down and concentrate on maintaining his health. The basic components you need to be mindful of are sleep, a healthy diet, and plenty of hydration. Apart from those, add some form of physical exercise to his daily routine. Whether it is riding his bike, playing at the park, or engaging in any sport he likes, he needs to stay physically fit. Schedule some downtime into his daily routine too. At the end of the day, give him some time to decompress and relax. Another simple aspect of his lifestyle you need to concentrate on is spending time outdoors. Encourage him to spend some time outdoors, whether it is to play or relax.

All the simple strategies discussed in this section make you a mindful parent while helping your child tackle his anxiety. Start incorporating the suggestions slowly into your parenting practices. It will take conscious effort and consistency, but your efforts will be worth it.

CHAPTER NINE

How to Help Your Child Manage

Fears

Fears are an inescapable part of human nature. Regardless of whether you are old or young, we all have our fears. They are an unavoidable part of childhood too. Whether it is hiding under the blankets when lightning strikes, behind the couch during a thunderstorm, or hiding from the boogeyman in the closet, children are scared of different things. Here is one scenario that sounds quite familiar to parents—it is time for your little one to go to bed. You have performed all the nightly routines, read him a bedtime story, tucked him in for a good night's sleep, and as you are about to switch off the light, he says, "Mommy can I have another glass of water?" or "Can I have five minutes before I sleep?" Why is the child doing all this? Perhaps he's scared of sleeping alone! All this is normal.

When your child is scared, the parental instant might be to comfort him. Reassure him there are no monsters in the closet, there is no boogeyman, and so on. Ideally, refrain from doing this. You might want to comfort him, but in the long run, this is not an ideal way to go about parenting him. Instead of teaching him to overcome his fears, you are merely fueling them. It might be quite cute if a three-year-old is worried about a monster under her bed, but if a 13-year-old does this, it's not age-appropriate. The best gift any parent can give to their kid is self-confidence. If you want to raise a confident child who is not always anxious, you need to reduce parental intervention. A little less parental intervention means more independence and confidence as he grows up. He will also feel more in control of his thoughts, feelings and emotions. In the section, let's look at some simple practices you can follow to help your child manage his fears.

Fill in the Missing Pieces

Children are still trying to understand the ways of the world. Only now are they beginning to comprehend the relationship between cause and effect. This relationship isn't obvious to them yet, and they are slowly learning. For instance, a child might be scared that if he plays too close to the vacuum cleaner, he will be sucked into it. It might seem quite obvious to an adult, but not so much to a child. By filling in the missing pieces of information, you help him get a better understanding of what is happening and the reasons for the same. For instance, you can show him how the vacuum cleaner works. Tell him that a button might be picked up by the machine but a shoe or a stuffed toy will not. So, obviously, a person cannot be sucked into it. Offering information helps the child rationalize what is happening. It can reduce their fears and anxieties too.

Concentrate on the Present

Most of the fears and anxieties children harbor are a combination of the past and the future. For instance, if a child is scared of dogs, it is probably because of a past incident where he was either chased by one or was barked at. This probably scared him. His brain might create a relationship between this past and a future incident such as a dog bite. Now, your child has not experienced it, yet his brain believes it can happen. This is the reason for his fear. By pulling him back to the present, you are preventing his brain from getting over-excited and worried about the future. This is especially true when your child starts generalizing different fears. Even though the incidents might seem similar, generalization is harmful. By teaching him the difference between different things, it reduces the intensity of the fear.

Don't Overreact

Whatever you do, do not overreact. Don't dismiss or invalidate your child's fears. Whatever he's feeling, it is quite real for him. For instance, if your kid is scared there is a monster hiding in the closet or under his bed, scooping him up and comforting him merely reinforces the presence of fear. Unknowingly, you are conveying the message that there is something to be scared of. Apart from this, you are also sending him a message that he will be safe in your arms. So the next time he is scared, he will expect you to pick him up. This shouldn't be his go-to solution whenever he's scared. A cuddle can be a reward, but it shouldn't be a reward for an avoidant behavior. Instead of comforting him, gently talk to him about what is happening. If he's scared of the sound the balloon makes when it pops, tell him what happened. After this, empathize with the fact that he got scared when the balloon popped. Talking about fear takes away its power. It will also make him more comfortable to approach you in the future and talk about his fears.

Storytelling Helps

Regardless of how irrational your child's fear or anxiety might seem, there is usually a rational story behind that fear. Any generalization he draws between different fears is automatic. A common generalization is "all dogs are bad" or "all dogs will hurt me." A simple way to interrupt this generalization is by focusing on the initial event that led to this manifestation. Stories are a part of our life. We use them to connect with others, heal, and expand our horizons and knowledge.

The right hemisphere of the brain is responsible for all your emotions and memories while the left hemisphere is the center for logic, factual details, and rationalization. Both these sides need to work in tandem or else you will experience the feeling of disconnection. A simple way to reestablish the link between both these hemispheres is via storytelling. The right brain usually becomes quite dominant whenever you experience any fear. This reaction is automatic. By reintroducing the left brain into the picture, intense fear is slowly replaced by rationalization. To do this, you need to consciously work on reintroducing the left brain by encouraging your child to tell his story. Next time, if your child says he is scared of dogs or all dogs are out to get him, ask him why he feels so. Encourage him to narrate the first incident that led to this fear. If he says something like, "I know dogs are dangerous because I've seen it," or "Dogs can hurt people," it is his right brain that is talking.

Once your child has narrated his story, encourage the participation of his right hemisphere by asking him specific questions. Ask him about what he felt during the experience or the different feelings he experiences whenever he is in a similar situation. If you see that your child is visibly scared or frightened while talking about his fears, state it. When you name an emotion, emotional intensity reduces. By encouraging a conversation about how his fears came into being, their power over him will reduce. When you talk about something that bothers you, the problem seems simpler and easier. If you don't talk about a specific experience or your child avoids talking about it, sooner or later those unprocessed thoughts and feelings will manifest themselves differently. If such unprocessed thoughts come to the forefront, they can manifest as anxiety. They might also present themselves as nightmares or recurring dreams. To avoid all this, try the simple activity of storytelling.

Reworking the Association

Fears are associated with feelings and memories. If these fears are intense, they are automatically associated with powerful feelings, emotions, and memories that are often bad. By reworking this association, you can reduce the fear your child feels. Concentrate on reworking the association by forming a new relationship with these fears. Instead of bad feelings and memories, replace them with fun and relaxing activities. For instance, if your child is extremely scared of thunderstorms, start by acknowledging his fears. Let him know it is normal and validated. After this, it is time to redirect him towards fun and relaxing activities such as watching a movie, coloring, or even listening to music. Once he's ready, you can turn it into a joke. Whenever there is lightning or thunder, someone has to crack a funny joke or play a peppy song. By doing this, you are essentially eliminating the scary thoughts or feelings and memories while replacing them with positive associations. After a while, this reduces the negative associations and replaces them with positive feelings that your child welcomes.

Stepladder Technique

This is a common technique used in therapy to reduce and overcome fears. It is based on the idea of gradually and gently exposing your child to an object or situation he's scared of. This slow and gradual exposure reduces his sensitivity to the trigger of fear and helps teach them a better response. When a child is scared of something, the object or situation seems quite scary and overwhelming. In such scenarios, your child would want to avoid said trigger as much as he possibly can. By slowly familiarizing him with the trigger, it increases his confidence. He will also feel less helpless and more empowered when faced with his fears. One thing you should remember while using this technique is to be slow and gradual. Remember the mantra" slow and steady wins the race" while using the stepladder technique. If your child is not yet ready, don't push him more than he can handle. It will prove counterproductive. Here are the simple steps you need to follow to use the stepladder technique.

Talk to Your Child

Before you implement this plan, you must discuss it with your kid. Unless he is on board with this plan, it will not work. After all, he is the hero of the story. You should also reassure him that he has complete control over what will be done and when to stop. This reassurance helps improve his confidence while facing the fear. Also, don't forget to remind him that you will never do anything that would harm him or his safety.

Let's assume that your child is really scared of dogs. Now, the idea is to help this fear and eliminate it if possible. To do this, it's time to start a conversation about dogs. Start by telling him you understand he's scared of dogs and the reasons why he's scared of them. After this, tell him not all dogs are generally scary. Your child might be worried that any dog he comes across will hurt him. His brain might start sounding alarm bells. Reassure and empathize that you understand his worries. Tell him it is not his fault for thinking so. Talk to him about how he feels when he's scared and how the fear controls him. Remind him that he's the boss of his brain. He can tell his brain what it needs to think.

Before you start explaining what the stepladder is, tell him you both will not be doing anything he doesn't want to. Don't forget to reassure him that you both will never do anything that can harm him. At the same time, remind him he needs to show a little courage to tackle his fear. Reassure him once again that the decision is truly his. Never underestimate the importance of reassurance while reframing what your child feels. After this, it is time to explain how this technique will work.

Explanation Time
Even if your child isn't fully on board with the idea yet, he might be slightly curious or fascinated by what you have in mind. Once he is open to listening to how this technique works, start talking about it. Perhaps you can use an example of something children are usually scared of but your kid is not. Constantly remind him there will always be an out and you can stop working on this technique whenever he wants. If you force him to do something or if he feels forced to, his fight-or-flight response will kick in and the fear can turn into anxiety. If this happens, his brain will forget about all logical reasoning and explanations. Instead, it will only receive information that he needs to get away from the situation and avoid it.

Talk to your child calmly and reassuringly. Start with an example of something that other kids are usually scared of, such as heights. Tell him that whatever you are saying is just an explanation and it doesn't mean he needs to follow it. This conversation can go something like this: "Do you know that a lot of children are scared of heights? Well, imagine how scary slippery slides might be for them. Imagine all the fun they are missing out on because they are scared of heights! What do you think such a child can do to make himself feel more comfortable with the slippery slide? How can he get used to being higher on the ladder?"

When you ask your child these questions, chances are he'll come up with a couple of answers. Keep an open mind to all the answers your child has, regardless of how quirky they sound. The idea of this process is to help him plan and analyze the activity at hand. This simple process helps strengthen all the different connections in his prefrontal cortex responsible for keeping his brain calm during anxiety.

Now, your child might have some interesting responses. Perhaps the most common response is, "Why doesn't the child try climbing one step at a time? Once he gets used to it, he can climb a little higher!" If your child comes up with this, your job just becomes a lot easier. On the other hand, chances are your child might also say something along the lines of, "If he's so scared of heights, stay away from slippery slides altogether. He doesn't need them!" Before you start shaking your head in resignation, accept your child's answer and offer some positive prompting. Perhaps you can suggest that the child in the hypothetical scenario should take it one step at a time and see how he feels.

Make It a Little Personal

If your child understands the idea of slow, gentle, or gradual exposure, start talking to him about his fears. Ask him what he would like to do to tackle these fears. Before you make any suggestions, ask him what he would be okay with. Try to understand that something is truly problematic only when that prevents him from leading his life like he's supposed to. If required, offer gentle prompts. Instead of telling him that he is suffering from anxiety or getting into its nuances, why don't you ask him how he would feel if he was not worried all the time? This can be a conversation starter. While talking about this, reassure him that he's quite brave and he has the power to stop his worries.

Simplify It

Fear can be quite overwhelming. A simple way to make it seem more manageable is by breaking it into smaller steps and worries. You and your child should be equally involved in this process. His willingness to commit to the suggestions or implement any of the proposed ideas is dependent on his level of involvement. Ensure the first step to tackle the fear is quite easy and it's something your child can do independently.

For instance, if your child is worried about sleeping on his own, work with him to create a plan of action. Perhaps the first step can be to leave the night light on for a while longer. You can stay with him for another 10 minutes before going to your room, or even check on him once every 10 minutes. Once he has cleared this stage, increase the time limit of checking on him to 20 minutes. Do this slowly until your child can successfully sleep through the night. It is doable, but it is not an overnight process. It will take plenty of time and attention. In the meanwhile, be patient.

Let us go back to the earlier example of a child who is scared of dogs. Now, you need to establish a simplified stepladder that can be used to conquer the fear of dogs. The easiest step should be at the bottom of the ladder while the hardest is at the top. If the child is scared of dogs, the first step can be to look at pictures of dogs. The second step might be to touch a soft toy and play with it. The third step can be watching a movie about a happy and friendly dog. The fourth step might be to stand in front of a dog without getting scared. The fifth step can be touching the dog, and the sixth step can be holding the dog for a while longer. Once the child is comfortable with a small dog, he can be encouraged to repeat the same process with a bigger dog.

The Rule About Small Steps

While breaking the fear into different steps, the distance between the two steps needs to be quite small. If the steps are too far apart, he can get overwhelmed. The smaller the distance, the easier it is for the child to move ahead. For instance, in the previous example, if the first step is to look at pictures of dogs and the second step is to hold a real dog, the chances of anxiety creeping in are quite high.

Don't Be In a Rush
Never forget that you are dealing with a child. Take as much time as he needs to comfortably make his way through the stepladder. Don't be in a rush. This is not a process that can be rushed. If you try to rush it, you will worsen your child's fear or anxiety. Don't forget to congratulate your child whenever he takes a step. Positive reinforcement and feedback will increase motivation to try the next step. If he needs a little push, offer encouragement, but don't be forceful. Forcing your child to do something he's not yet ready to do will increase anxiety.

CHAPTER TEN

How to Teach Positive Thinking to Tackle Anxiety

When your child's worrying thoughts become excessive, his ability to cope with them reduces. From poor sleep to reduced attention and reluctance to do things outside his comfort zone, there are different problems associated with anxiety. A powerful technique you can use to help your child overcome his worries is to teach him to think realistically. The process is quite simple. You essentially teach him how to identify a worrying thought, look for any evidence to support the thought, and if there is no evidence, replace it with something more realistic. This is an essential part of cognitive-behavioral therapy discussed in the previous chapter. It teaches him to reframe all his negative thoughts, behaviors, and emotions and transform them into something more positive and realistic.

It might sound like positive thinking, but it is not. The worrying thoughts are replaced with realistic ones instead of positive ones. If you want to teach your child this technique, here are the steps you should follow.

The first step is perhaps the most difficult one. Start by identifying his thoughts. Tell him thoughts are nothing more than words we say to ourselves. These words don't have to be said out loud, but we think them. An average brain thinks thousands of thoughts daily. Most of these are automatic and are similar to the blowing wind. Merely identifying a thought can be quite empowering for the child.

You can try playing some simple games to help your child identify his thoughts. For instance, if you are watching a movie, cartoon, or even looking at pictures in a book, ask him what those people might be thinking. Encourage him to guess what those characters might be thinking. Alternatively, you can give him a situation or an event and ask what a specific person might be feeling. For instance, if he is scared of dogs, ask him what his beloved character would think or feel in a situation when a dog is present in front of him. Ask him to draw what he's thinking or name the thought.

Depending on his age, you can also go ahead and explain the connection between our thoughts, feelings, and behaviors. For instance, any thought that worries us can cause butterflies in our stomachs. This feeling increases the temptation to avoid the situation that's causing the worry. You must spend some time and help him accurately identify his worry. If he's scared of the dark, chances are he will tell you he is experiencing an emotion instead of the thought. A sentence such as "I'm scared of the dark" identifies his feelings. The feeling is fear. You will need to probe a little deep and ask him what exactly about the dark scares him. This helps identify the worrying thought.

Once he has identified his worry, encourage him to gather the required evidence to support his thought. Tell him he's playing the role of a detective and looking for clues to support his thought. You can also ask him simple questions in this activity.

If he is scared of the dark, ask him, "What about the dark scares you?" If he says he's worried about a boogeyman in the closet or a monster under his bed, ask him how likely is that a boogeyman is present in the closet or a monster is hiding under his bed. Ask him how he will feel about the same worry a couple of weeks later. Or maybe you can ask him what his favorite character or even best friend would do in a similar situation.

After going through this activity, chances are your child's worry is not founded in reality. If that's the case, you need to teach him to replace this worrying thought with something more realistic. If he hears a creepy sound right before going to bed, instead of assuming it's a monster under the bed, ask him what it can be. If he's struggling to answer, offer some helpful suggestions such as the rustling of the wind or any other noise coming from outside.

Once you have followed all these steps, chances are your child's fear will have been replaced with something more realistic. This is one activity you need to perform repeatedly to help him overcome his fears. Changing his thinking pattern is not an overnight process. To do this, you need to regularly talk to him about what he's feeling and what is going on in his head. Regular check-ins will encourage him to open up about his worries. If you are an empathetic listener, he will talk more about his worries without the fear of judgment.

Whenever possible, talk to him about emotions and correctly identify his thoughts. Encourage him to tell you what exactly he is worried about instead of stating his emotions.

After this, teach him to think more realistically with examples. An ideal way to do this is by modeling the behavior you want him to learn. After all, parents are a child's first role model. By incorporating fun activities and games into this process, you make realistic thinking fun and exciting. It's also a great way to bond with your little one.

Chapter eleven

Self-Soothing Techniques for Kids with Anxiety

It's not likely that you will be with your child whenever he experiences anxiety. So, you need to equip him with certain skills and tools he can use whenever anxiety strikes. Let's look at some simple activities your child can perform anywhere and at any time to gain better control of his senses and relax.

Deep Breathing

When your child is anxious, his breathing becomes rapid and shallow. A simple way to counteract this anxiety response is by regulating his breathing. Encourage your child to take calm, slow, and deep breaths whenever he's anxious. This reduces the feeling of stress. The activity he needs to perform is quite simple. Ask him to breathe slowly and deeply through his nose, hold onto this breath for a second or two before exhaling through his mouth. Encourage him to repeat this process five to 10 times or until he feels calmer. According to the research conducted by Valentina Perciavalle et al. (2017), deep breathing reduces stress in any situation.

A Mental Vacation

A simple way to help your child let go of his anxiety is by encouraging him to take a mental vacation. Even if he cannot physically distance himself from the stressor, ask him to close his eyes and think of his favorite place. Whether it is the beach, park, or the mountains, ask him to visualize his favorite place. If not, ask him to think about his favorite memory—perhaps the family vacation or even a visit to Disneyland. By visualizing his favorite destination, his anxious mind will become calm. Depending on your child's age, ask him to make his visualization quite realistic. From how he felt on a specific day or at that place to the different smells, sounds, and sights, encourage him to think about all of it.

Head to Toe Relaxations

According to the research conducted by Maryam Zargardzadeh (2014), progressive muscle relaxation reduces anxiety. Even though the subjects of this study were nursing students, there's no reason why it wouldn't stand true for kids. A method to do relaxation or progressive relaxation is the next step of deep breathing. Ask your child to find a quiet spot for himself and place a hand on his tummy and another on his chest. Ask him to close his eyes and keep breathing slowly and deeply until his entire body feels calm. This reduces muscle tension and calms his mind. When his body is physically calm, his mind will slowly calm down too.

Holding on Tight

Anxiety triggers muscle tension. This is an involuntary consequence of the stress response. A simple way to help your child counteract this involuntary muscle tension is by holding on tight or squeezing something. Whether it is modeling clay, a stuffed animal, or a stress ball, the action of holding tight reduces tension. It also diverts your child's mind from the anxious thought and helps him concentrate on something else.

A Positive Thought

In the previous chapter, you were introduced to different steps you can follow to teach your child realistic thinking. Now, it is time to encourage him to replace his worrying and negative thoughts with positive ones. If your child is anxious about meeting new people or scared of trying something new, ask him to replace these thoughts with positive ones. For instance, if he believes that he cannot do something, encourage him to think, "I can do it," or "I am strong enough to do it." If he keeps repeating these positive thoughts like a mantra, it distracts the mind and encourages relaxation.

A Little Movement

According to the research conducted by Elizabeth Anderson et al. (2013), physical movement and activity reduce anxiety and stress response. Whenever your child is anxious, encourage him to engage in a little physical activity. Whether it is jumping on the spot for a minute or two or running three laps in the yard or the playground, some form of physical movement helps. When he gets his body moving, feel-good endorphins are released that reduce the presence of cortisol in his body.

Listening to Music

Music has a therapeutic and calming effect on the mind. According to the research conducted by Myrian V. Thoma et al. (2013), listening to music reduces the intensity and duration of the stress response. The next time your child feels anxious, encourage him to listen to his favorite song. If he cannot do this, ask him to sing or hum his favorite song. If possible, an impromptu dance party in the living room will act as a great stress buster.

Apart from all these self-soothing techniques, there's another important tip you need to remember. Dear parents, be a good role model for your child. How you deal with your anxiety and stress sets the tone for how your child learns to cope with them. The next time you feel overwhelmed, anxious, or worried, explain what you're feeling. Instead of letting your emotions get the better of you and acting out, calmly state what you are feeling. When you are anxious, having an outburst is quite likely. Instead of an outburst, say something like, "I have so many things to complete and I'm worried that I cannot complete. I just need to take a break for a minute until I feel better."

Chapter twelve

Anxiety Relapse

The joy of truly knowing that your child is free from symptoms of anxiety and can manage his emotions and feelings positively is quite exhilarating. No one will want their child's anxiety to relapse. While your child is learning to manage his anxiety, you might be waiting for the other shoe to drop. Bracing yourself for any hint of anxiety to return is anxiety-inducing for parents. Unfortunately, there are instances when there can be a relapse. Even if your child has been coping incredibly well with his anxiety, the chances of a relapse are possible. It can be quite exhausting and overwhelming to think you need to repeat everything you've done until now all over again. So, it's always better to prepare yourself for the reasons that can trigger anxiety relapse. When you know what needs to be avoided, taking corrective action before it manifests into a problem becomes easier. In this chapter, you will learn about some causes of relapse of anxiety in children and what to do in case of a relapse.

Causes of a Relapse

It might have been a while since your child faced his original fear. All of a sudden, an event or an occurrence triggers his fear again. Let's assume that your child had an intense fear of spiders and managed to overcome it. After a couple of months, you are all watching some movie about spiders and it triggers his phobia again. Or perhaps your child was dealing with separation anxiety. He managed to overcome it, and after a while, there was an unforeseeable circumstance where you were separated from your child. This can trigger a relapse of his fear. There can also be an environmental change in the household that is traumatic for the child. Dealing with an illness, the death of a loved one, or shifting to a new place can be quite stressful and anxiety-inducing for children. If any such events occur, the chances of relapse also increase.

If there are any significant changes in the situation surrounding the fear, there can be a relapse. For instance, your child might have been quite scared about starting elementary school. From social anxiety to separation anxiety, he experienced it all. He managed his anxiety and got used to the school. Everything was going well until he had to start middle school. As the date approached, his anxiety returned. This is quite possible.

There can be situations where your child's anxiety levels are better but he still prefers to play it safe. For instance, he might be quite anxious about whether all the doors and windows are locked and secured at night. He might have learned to stop indulging in this obsessive behavior or compulsion of checking the doors and windows every night. That said, it doesn't mean he will not ask for reassurance that everything is properly taken care of. If he constantly asks for this reassurance even though he is not engaging in the compulsive behavior, it is a sign his anxiety has returned.

Any situation of unrelated anxiety or stress can trigger his previous anxieties. Simply put, when your child faces a traumatic incident or a frightening situation, his anxiety can return. For instance, a child who has learned to manage his fear of dogs and gets over it can have a relapse upon hearing that one of his friends was bitten by a dog.

What to Do Now?

If you are working with your child to reduce his anxiety and it returns, it can be quite stressful for you. Regardless of the combination of treatments you are using to help your child manage his anxiety, whenever it relapses, you need to go back to the basics. Anxiety can be quite stubborn and the fears are never truly forgotten. Relapse is similar to an old memory which is once again remembered vividly. During a relapse, the goal is not to reduce your child's anxiety but disprove his fear once again. Once the fear goes away, the anxiety will also reduce.

It's time to go back to the basics. Start identifying all those beliefs your child is harboring and paying attention to once again. It's time to challenge all of them. Practice the different tips discussed in the previous chapter about helping your child face and manage his fears. If you believe any specific incident or situation is triggering his anxiety, give him a break from it. Once your child has managed to identify his fear, you can start again. In this section, let's look at simple tips you can follow if your child has a relapse.

The first step is you have to be calm. Do not lose your patience and do not get upset with your child. It is incredibly frustrating for him to go through the same things he has already lived through. It can be frustrating for you and it is understandable. It is equally understandable that your child is frustrated too. You need to stay calm right now.

Concentrate on teaching him to develop his confidence. Give him the confidence and support required to keep going without giving up. He's counting on you for all of this. Don't lose hope; be his cheerleader.

If one of his previous fears has become active now, it is time to face it. The sooner you accept it, the easier it is to face the fear. Challenge his fears instead of avoiding or ignoring them. Encourage your child to do the same. It might seem easy to ignore or avoid the fear because it is triggering his anxiety, but don't do this. Reassure him that you are there with him and he can manage this fear too.

While you are helping your child face his fear, ensure that you don't stop once it eases. Instead, it's time to go all the way. Relapses are common. Things can get better, but it doesn't mean the anxiety goes away. If you realize his anxiety is once again interfering with his daily life and preventing him from living his life to the fullest, it's time to tackle it. Face all the fears, revisit them, and help him challenge them. Follow the tips discussed in the previous chapters to do this.

Apart from this, consult his healthcare provider about the relapse immediately. If required, restart cognitive behavioral therapy once again. Whether it is therapy or medication, ensure you get him the required help

Chapter thirteen

Parents Should Not Pass on Their Anxiety to Kids

Consider this scenario. A parent was trying to get her kid to his softball practice. Before leaving the house, she got an important call from work that delayed her attempts to get to the practice on time. She was anxious about her work and didn't check whether her kid was wearing his softball uniform or not. On the way to the practice, she noticed he was not dressed for practice. She felt frustrated and overwhelmed and ended up shouting at her kid for not being ready on time.

What do you think is wrong in this situation? The mother was unknowingly projecting her anxiety and frustration on her kid. She didn't make sure whether he was dressed for the practice or not before leaving home. She was transferring her anxiety to her kid, who became the unintended victim of her outburst.

Now, consider the same situation from the child's perspective. The child might believe he was shouted at because he wasn't dressed properly. Whenever he needs to go out, he might become anxious wondering whether or not he is dressed according to what his parents want. He might also develop some irrational fears associated with this incident. In the situation mentioned above, the child was not scared of his mother, but of the negative reaction. He might believe he had upset his mother. Children expect their parents to be their rock. Seeing their solid pillar of support crumble under pressure sends the wrong message.

What is the moral of this story? The moral is quite simple— don't pass your anxiety to your kid. Children take their cues from their parents. They look to the parents for information about interpreting ambiguous situations. When your child witnesses you in an utter state of anxiety, it is unsettling for him. If your go-to response in a situation is to become scared, fearful, or anxious, your child will think such situations are unsafe. Despite your best intentions, you are unknowingly communicating your stress and anxiety to the kid. Not a lot of adults realize this, but children are quick learners and good observers. How you present yourself in a stressful situation will teach him his basic stress responses. If you are dealing with any anxiety, ensure that you don't feel guilty about it. Experiencing or living with anxiety is not easy. Understanding that it's not your fault and accepting the situation is the first step to tackle it.

The transmission of anxiety from a parent to a kid is inevitable. The second thing you need to do is ensure that you don't do this. So, you need to learn to manage your anxiety first. You cannot be of much help to your child while crumbling under pressure. By letting your emotions get the best of you, you are setting a poor example for him.

When you're struggling with your anxiety, keeping calm becomes difficult. You can also talk about what you are feeling when overwhelmed by your emotions. Learning stress management techniques according to your specific needs and requirements is helpful. When you learn to tolerate stress, you are showing your child how to cope with stressful situations or uncertainty and doubt. An important part of treating children with anxiety is to teach stress tolerance to parents. This is a simultaneous process that works in both directions. When you set a good example of how to manage stress, you are essentially showing your child how to stay calm.

The different stress management techniques you use can be used by your child whenever he feels anxious. For instance, thinking rationally becomes incredibly difficult during stressful times. A simple exercise you can use to concentrate on your breathing is something your child can also practice whenever he feels anxious. Another technique you can use is the rationalization of thoughts. If something is overwhelming or stressing you, communicate about it to your child. Once you state the problem, talk about scary situations and the likely outcome. Ask your child, how likely do you think the situation is bound to come true? Practicing realistic thinking is a great stress-relieving activity.

While dealing with a stressful situation, pay extra attention to your facial expressions and body language. Body language communicates more than words ever can. If your face looks tensed, scared, or worried, your child will pick on it. Learn to choose your words carefully, regulate the intensity of your emotions, and pay attention to your facial expressions. Your child is a sponge and he's picking up on everything you are saying and doing.

You might not want your child to see you during an anxious situation, but don't try to suppress your emotions. Avoiding any issue and emotion suppression are two things that you need to avoid at all costs. This teaches unhealthy and maladaptive coping mechanisms to your kid. Instead of suppressing what you are feeling, talk to your child about what is causing your anxiety. When he knows you're stressed and are working on reducing that stress or maintaining a positive outlook, it becomes easier for him to understand what to do. Seeing a parent cope with stress is okay and healthy for a child. At the same time, you should also explain why you chose to react the way you did.

For instance, let's say you lost your cool because you were worried about not getting your child to school on time. Once he is back home from school or when you feel calmer, talk to him about the stressful situation. Tell him you were quite anxious in the morning when he was getting late for school and you managed your anxiety by yelling. At the same time, also tell him that this was not an ideal reaction. Teach him better ways to cope with stress instead of yelling. You can set a good example by talking about anxiety. This gives your child the permission to express and feel his stress. Acknowledgment goes a long way in helping your child manage anxiety.

You cannot avoid stressful situations and circumstances in life. Regardless of how hard you try, stress is a part of life. So, you need to create a plan of action to deal with stressful situations and triggers. If you get stressed when deadlines are fast approaching or anxious if your child doesn't go to bed on time, talk to him about it. It's always better to have a reasonable conversation and create a plan of action that can be implemented instead of giving in to your emotions.

Learn to disengage. At times, prolonging a conversation does more harm than good. If you believe a specific situation is worsening the stress you are experiencing, disengage. For instance, if you are unable to deal with the anxiety of dropping your child at school, ask your partner, friend, or another family member to step in for you. Learning your limits is as important as working on overcoming your anxieties and fears. If you start giving in to your anxiety whenever you need to drop your child at school, it conveys the wrong message. Sooner or later, your child will form an unhealthy association that being dropped off at school or going to school is an act that upsets his parents. You don't want your child to have such unhealthy associations. So, become mindful of your reactions and responses to stress.

Whenever you start to feel a little overwhelmed in the presence of your child, permit yourself to take a break from it. For instance, if you're getting stressed about a work-related issue and your child is in the same room, step away from the room. Before you do this, tell him you need a break for five minutes and will be back within five minutes. By explaining what you are experiencing and what you plan to do, it gives him a better idea of what's expected of him. It also shows him better anxiety coping mechanisms.

Dear parents, you need a support system in place to help your anxiety too. You are your child's support system, so who is yours? Whether it is your spouse, partner, friends, family members, or colleagues at work, you need people to depend on in moments of extreme anxiety or stress. If not, you can join a support group, seek professional help, or anything else that calms you down. Learning to manage your anxiety can work wonders for a child's anxiety. Instead of fueling his fears and anxiety, manage your own. It is okay to take a break, it is okay to ask for help, and it is certainly okay to make time for yourself. Practicing a little self-care can work wonders for your health. You will learn more about self-care techniques in the next chapter.

CHAPTER FOURTEEN

Self-Care Tips for Parents

Once you are a parent, your life undergoes a major transformation. You have now entered a role that never really ends. Whether it is a young child, teenager, or adult, you never stop playing the role of a parent. Taking care of your child will always be a priority. As parents, we're all constantly worried about their health, finances, success, social life, and other achievements. Apart from this, we also worry about their overall happiness. All this is quite normal and it is a part of your job description.

You are a parent, but there are other roles you need to play too. Whether it is your professional or personal commitments, you need to manage those as well. As an adult, you will have your own set of worries. From finances to relationships, your job, health, and everything else, there is a lot to manage. At times, all this becomes incredibly overwhelming. You probably realize all the different things your child worries about and steps you can use to promote their self-care. It is time to concentrate on self-care. When there are so many obligations and responsibilities you need to juggle, self-care is the first thing that goes out of the window. A common reason why parents are constantly overwhelmed, tired, or even anxious is because they have no time to take care of themselves. In your attempt to take care of everyone in your life, you are compromising on yourself. Stop doing this.

Until now, the importance of being a mindful parent while dealing with an anxious child was repeatedly stressed. Well, it's not just children who need to be taken care of, but even you need to do this for yourself. Self-care is important. Taking care of your own needs ensures that you are your best self while dealing with your child. Parenting your anxious little one can be an all-consuming job. When you are constantly stressed and worried about him, it will sooner or later take a toll on you. This is one of the reasons why you need to prioritize your health and wellbeing too. Here are some simple suggestions you can use to practice self-care.

Start Prioritizing

You are a human being and not superhuman. Let go of the notion that you can do everything. The first step is to accept your human nature. It is okay to let go and not do everything. If you have multiple obligations, start prioritizing. Most of your priorities might involve your child, family members, and other loved ones. Take some time, find a quiet spot, and make a list of all your obligations and responsibilities. From this list, select one or two obligations that are the most important for you. For instance, you might like knitting, gardening, painting, or watching movies. Whatever it is, select two items from this list and prioritize them. If there's someone else in the house you can share your responsibilities with, divide your responsibilities.

Once you have your list of priorities, ensure that you concentrate on them. Don't compromise on self-care for the sake of everything else. Unless you are at your 100%, you cannot be of much help to anyone. Give yourself the permission to enjoy life and take care of yourself. It is okay to worry about your child, but your worries become more manageable and less overwhelming when you are physically, mentally, and emotionally refreshed.

Take Some Time Out

Yes, you have hundreds of responsibilities to manage. When there are so many duties that need to be performed, 24 hours might not seem sufficient. Remember the simple announcement on airplanes about putting on your oxygen mask first before helping others. You become better at taking care of others when you take care of yourself. The good thing about self-care is it doesn't have to be a chore that takes up hours together. 20 minutes daily for self-care will do. Whether it is 20 minutes to read, engaging in your hobbies, talking to someone, or taking a break, do whatever you want. You not only need a break but deserve it too. Plan your days such that you get some time for yourself. Don't feel guilty for taking time for self-care.

Spending Time With Your Loved Ones

A simple way to de-stress and let go of any unnecessary worries and feel better is by spending time with your loved ones. Humans have always thrived as groups. This is how civilizations were formed and societies created. We need others around us. We are not lone wolves. Whether it is your family, friends, or colleagues, spend some time with those who make you feel better. If you are swamped with taking care of your child, professional responsibilities, and personal obligations, you will become overwhelmed. If you believe you don't have as much time as you used to initially to go out and meet your friends, set up weekly phone calls. Set a day aside from your daily routines to spend time with those you love. You will feel better.

Schedule Fun Activities

Make a note of all the different activities you love and enjoy. Once you have this list ready, it's time to schedule some fun into your daily routine. Yes, you read it right. You need to schedule fun activities. It might sound contradictory that you need to plan for fun, but it works. There are several things you might enjoy. At times, even going over the list of different activities you enjoy tends to become stressful. After all, there are 24 hours per day at your disposal. If there are multiple things you want to do, you need to make time for it by planning. For instance, you might like reading, doing yoga, watching TV, baking, or even going for a leisurely walk. Why don't you plan your day such that you can include at least one of these activities daily? This is more doable than getting stressed looking at the list. At least this way you are doing something that you like.

Pamper Yourself

Dear parent, your child is not the only one that needs to be pampered. All children expect to be pampered. Whether it is staying up late to watch a movie or going out for occasional ice cream, these are all treats kids enjoy. Well, now it's time to do the same thing for yourself. Once in a while, pamper yourself. Whether it is getting a manicure-pedicure, going on a shopping spree, or even treating yourself to ice cream, do it. You need an occasional treat too. You deserve that!

Go Out

Getting out of the house shouldn't be synonymous with running errands, going to the grocery store, or dropping off laundry. You need to go out of the house and kitchen. Whether it is going for a walk or a long drive, spend some time outside the house. Don't restrict yourself to work or the house alone. Take a break to cool off. Heading outdoors helps break free of the confinements of daily life. Have a parent night out once a week or maybe every alternate week. If you schedule this into your daily routine, it becomes easier. Even your children will become more accommodating and understanding of your time to cool off. If you know you have to go out once a month, you can make alternate arrangements to take care of your kids. It will also give you something to look forward to. Do you count the days until you can go on a holiday or a vacation? Why do you do this? Because it gives you something to look forward to! Well, why don't you give yourself something to look forward to by scheduling some time off your usual parental responsibilities?

Organization Matters

A simple way to take care of yourself is by creating a schedule. When you stay on top of all your responsibilities and obligations, the stress associated with them melts away. For instance, if you're worried about your finances, spend some time and create a plan of action that helps restabilize your financial situation. Instead of worrying about it, you are doing something to tackle the stress. In all conversations about self-care, the importance of organizing is always emphasized. If your professional or personal life is in disarray, any stress you experience increases. If managing the necessities of daily life itself becomes stressful, you cannot find the time to relax. Whether you are using a to-do list, doing meal prep, or organizing your closet, find an efficient way to bring some order into your life. When there is order, chaos goes away. The lack of chaos automatically eliminates stress. Why worry about tackling stress if you can prevent it from cropping up altogether?

Concentrate On Your Future

When all your time and energy goes toward taking care of your children, planning for the future, and securing it, you might not have any time to think about yourself. This is one common mistake most parents make. We get so caught up in our responsibilities we forget to plan for our future. As your child grows, he will become more independent. It means you will have more time for yourself. The best way to ensure your future is something you desire by planning for it. It means you need to think about your lifestyle, career changes (if any), and your dreams. Start saving for your future. Whether it is retirement or a world trip, you need to concentrate on saving for it too. Planning and preparation are important.

Your Health is Important

Never ignore your health for the sake of others. You need to take care of your physical, mental, and emotional wellbeing. Whether it is an anxious child at home or any other common cause of worry, your health needs to be a priority too. Don't skip your doctor's appointments! Concentrate on getting sufficient sleep at night, consuming a healthy diet, and exercising regularly. When you practice healthy lifestyle habits, you are setting a good example for your kid to follow. After all, most of the behaviors children pick up are from the adults around. So, why don't you start modeling some good behavior?

For instance, how do you respond to stress? If your answer is to get overwhelmed, have an emotional outburst, or do something along these lines, you are setting a poor example. If you want your child to manage stress, you need to set a good example. Always remember, practice before you preach.

By following the simple and practical tips given in this chapter, you can ensure that self-care becomes a priority too. Let go of any guilt associated with spending time for yourself. You deserve it too.

CONCLUSION

We all have our own set of worries and insecurities. Whether it is an adult or a young child, fears, insecurities, and worries are common. Children are trying to make sense of the world around them. They slowly understand the relationship between cause and effect. Childhood fears are incredibly common. Whether it is the fear of the boogeyman or the dark, your child will be afraid of one thing or the other. By now, you might have realized how common anxiety is these days. Children and adults alike suffer from anxiety caused by different reasons. From biological factors to environmental conditioning and atmosphere at home, different factors can cause childhood anxiety. This anxiety can present itself as social anxiety, panic attacks, excessive worry or fear, or even separation anxiety. The first step towards tackling all this is to understand what causes these anxieties and what triggers them.

In this book, you were introduced to what anxiety means, how it influences the brain, chemical imbalances that result in anxiety, and signs and symptoms to watch out for. Even though fears are common, when these fears prevent your child from living his life to the fullest, they become problematic. Apart from considering regular treatment options for anxiety such as cognitive behavioral therapy or any other form of therapy, there are different things you can do to help alleviate his anxiety. One thing you're never supposed to do is swoop in and try to fix things. Ignore the parental instinct of trying to save the day for your child. The best thing you can do is teach him to manage his anxiety and regulate his thoughts. This is a great way to raise an independent and confident child. These valuable skills you equip him will stay with him all life long.

Parenting is a full-time job without any breaks or vacations. Whether it is a toddler or a teenager, you never stop being a parent. Worrying about your child's overall wellbeing is a part of a parent's job description. So, it is time for you to take corrective action and guide your child in the right direction. Several things cannot be regulated or even predicted in life. The good news is, anxiety can be managed and eliminated. It will take consistent effort, patience, conscious changes, and resilience, but your efforts will be worth it.

Knowingly or unknowingly, most parents feed their child's fears. They might also encourage their child to fuel his fears. These are two things you need to avoid. In this book, you were introduced to a list of desirable and undesirable responses you need to avoid while dealing with an anxious child. Instead, a favorable approach is to teach your child to manage, face, and overcome his fears. Whether you are using the stepladder approach or are reworking the negative associations with positive ones, there are different techniques you can use. Depending on your child and his temperament, choose one that works well for you.

Another tip all parents need to remember is to never force their child to do anything he isn't ready for. Even a seemingly simple activity might seem frightening to your child. Do not dismiss his worries and anxieties. Instead, acknowledge and validate his feelings. Start a healthy and honest conversation about anxiety. The thing about fears is, they lose their power once you start talking about them. Encourage your child to be forthcoming about his worries. It is your responsibility to ensure that your child can reach out to you in times of his need.

In this book, you were given all the information required to recognize the progress your child makes while preventing the chances of relapses, identifying his triggers and fears, and helping your child think realistically. By equipping him with the skills required to face the fear and fight, you are teaching him to plan for a better future. You are not alone in this situation. Dealing with your child's anxieties is not easy, but it is doable. Before you work on helping your child elevate his anxieties, ensure that you have all the information required. This is where this book steps into the picture. It will act as your guide every step of the way. Whenever in doubt, refer to the information and simple suggestions given in this book. It's not just your child's help that is important, concentrate on yourself too. Dear parent, you cannot be of much help to the child unless you are functioning effectively and efficiently. Follow the simple self-care suggestions given in this book and you will see a positive change.

While you implement these suggestions about tackling your child's fears or anxiety, ensure that you consider his comfort level too. All children are unique. So, what might work for one might not necessarily work for your kid. Don't get discouraged or disheartened. If something isn't working, try another route! There is no scientific guide to parenting. It is a process of trial and error. Don't mistake your child's introversion for anxiety. Understanding his personality, temperament, and development is important. If you push your child to do something he isn't ready for yet, it will backfire. You need to be his support system, pillar of strength, and cheerleader. Regulate your emotions, thoughts, and feelings before concentrating on your little one.

I understand the difficulties and tricky aspects of parenting an anxious child. All the suggestions discussed in this book are based on my personal experience. Through years of research and implementation, I have seen a positive change in my little one. I know he is shaping up to be a confident and independent teenager. Don't worry too much because I've got your back. Don't hesitate to reach out to your loved ones in the time of need. You don't have to go through this alone!

Now that you are equipped with all the information you need, it is time to implement the simple and practical suggestions and tips discussed in this book. One important thing you need to remember while implementing these suggestions is to be incredibly patient. Never lose your patience and stay calm and composed even when your child is anxious. After all, he's counting on you for strength and support during his anxious times. It will take a consistent and conscious effort to equip your little one with the skills and tools required to tackle anxiety. Helping your child lead an anxiety-free life is possible. Take the first step towards this goal and get started immediately.

Finally, if you have enjoyed reading this book and found it informative, take a couple of minutes and leave a review on Amazon! Your feedback can help several other parents who are in the same situation as you.

Thank you and all the best!

REFERENCES

All images sourced from Pixabay.

6 major types of anxiety disorders. (2019, July 10). CHOC Children's Blog.https://blog.chocchildrens.org/6-major-types-of-anxiety-disorders/

8 Myths About Anxiety in Children and Teens. (2019, July 7). Goodbye Anxiety, Hello Joy. https://goodbyeanxietyhellojoy.com/myths-about-anxiety/

10 Self-Care Tips for Parents. (2020, January 8). MGH Clay Center for Young Healthy Minds. https://www.mghclaycenter.org/parenting-concerns/10-self-care-tips-for-parents/

Anderson, E., & Shivakumar, G. (2013). Effects of Exercise and Physical Activity on Anxiety. Frontiers in Psychiatry, 4. https://doi.org/10.3389/fpsyt.2013.00027

Anxiety disorders Symptoms & Causes | Boston Children's Hospital. (n.d.). Www.childrens hospital.org. https://www.childrenshospital.org/conditions-and-treatments/conditions/a/anxiety-disorders/symptoms-and-causes

Childhood fears: What's common and how can you help?

- Children's Health. (2019). Childrens.com. https://www.childrens.com/health-wellness/childhood-fears

Cullens, A. (2017). 7 Effective Ways to Help Children Overcome Social Anxiety. Big Life Journal. https://biglifejournal.com/blogs/blog/help-children-overcome-social-anxiety-failure

Data and Statistics on Children's Mental Health. (2019, April 19). Centers for Disease Control and Prevention. https://www.cdc.gov/childrensmentalhealth/data.html#ref

Data and Statistics on Children's Mental Health | CDC. (2020, June 15). Centers for Disease Control and Prevention. https://www.cdc.gov/childrensmentalhealth/data.html#:~:text=7.4%25%20of%20children%20aged%203

Davies, M. N., Verdi, S., Burri, A., Trzaskowski, M., Lee, M., Hettema, J. M., Jansen, R., Boomsma, D. I., & Spector, T. D. (2015). Generalised Anxiety Disorder – A Twin Study of Genetic Architecture, Genome-Wide Association and Differential Gene Expression. PLOS ONE, 10(8), e0134865. https://doi.org/10.1371/journal.pone.0134865

Don't Argue With a Brain Glitch. (10 Do's and 5 Don'ts for Parents of Kids with OCD). (n.d.). OCD • Anxiety • Psychologists • Psychotherapists • Ontario. https://www.turningpointpsychology.ca/blog/children-with-ocd-guidelines-for-parents

Eapen, V. (2014). Developmental and mental health disorders: Two sides of the same coin. Asian Journal of Psychiatry, 8, 7–11. https://doi.org/10.1016/j.ajp.2013.10.007

Ehmke, R. (2016, March 10). Helping Children Cope After a Traumatic Event. Child Mind Institute; Child Mind Institute. https://childmind.org/guide/helping-children-cope-traumatic-event/

Ferguson, S. (2019, June 27). Is Anxiety Genetic? Healthline;

Healthline Media. https://www.healthline.com/health/mental-health/is-anxiety-genetic#symptoms

Ghandour, R. M., Sherman, L. J., Vladutiu, C. J., Ali, M. M., Lynch, S. E., Bitsko, R. H., & Blumberg, S. J. (2019). Prevalence and Treatment of Depression, Anxiety, and Conduct Problems in US Children. The Journal of Pediatrics, 206, 256-267.e3. https://doi.org/10.1016/j.jpeds.2018.09.021

Gomstyn, A. (n.d.). Kids and anxiety: What's normal, what's not. Aetna. https://www.aetna.com/health-guide/kids-anxiety-whats-normal-seek-help.html

Gottschalk, M. G., & Domschke, K. (2016). Novel developments in genetic and epigenetic mechanisms of anxiety. Current Opinion in Psychiatry, 29(1), 32–38. https://doi.org/10.1097/yco.0000000000000219

Gottschalk, M. G., & Domschke, K. (2017). Genetics of generalized anxiety disorder and related traits. Dialogues in Clinical Neuroscience, 19(2), 159–168. https://www.ncbi.nlm.nih.gov/pmc/articles/PMC5573560/

How to Ease Your Child's Separation Anxiety. (2019). HealthyChildren.org. https://www.healthychildren.org/English/ages-stages/toddler/Pages/Soothing-Your-Childs-Separation-Anxiety.aspx

Hurley, K. (2016). 10 Things Never to Say to Your Anxious Child - Pyscom.net. Psycom.net - Mental Health Treatment Resource since 1986. https://www.psycom.net/child-anxiety-things-never-to-say

Hurley, K. (2016). Helping Kids with Anxiety: Strategies to Help Anxious Children. Psycom.net - Mental Health Treatment Resource since 1986. https://www.psycom.net/help-kids-with-anxiety

Kelly, K. (2019, August 6). 8 Self-Soothing Techniques for

Your Young Child. Understood.org; Understood. https://www.understood.org/en/friends-feelings/managing-feelings/fear/8-self-soothing-techniques-for-your-young-child

Morris-Rosendahl, D. J. (2002). Are there anxious genes? Dialogues in Clinical Neuroscience, 4(3), 251–260. https://www.ncbi.nlm.nih.gov/pmc/articles/PMC3181683/

Panic attacks in children - tips for parents on how to help your child cope. (n.d.). Priory Group. https://www.priorygroup.com/blog/panic-attacks-in-children-tips-for-parents-on-how-to-help-your-child-cope

Perciavalle, V., Blandini, M., Fecarotta, P., Buscemi, A., Di Corrado, D., Bertolo, L., Fichera, F., & Coco, M. (2017). The role of deep breathing on stress. Neurological Sciences : Official Journal of the Italian Neurological Society and of the Italian Society of Clinical Neurophysiology, 38(3), 451–458. https://doi.org/10.1007/s10072-016-2790-8

Qin, S., Young, C. B., Duan, X., Chen, T., Supekar, K., & Menon, V. (2014). Amygdala Subregional Structure and Intrinsic Functional Connectivity Predicts Individual Differences in Anxiety During Early Childhood. Biological Psychiatry, 75(11), 892–900. https://doi.org/10.1016/j.biopsych.2013.10.006

Reeb-Sutherland, B. C. (2017). What Environmental Factors Contribute to the Development of Anxiety in Temperamentally Inhibited Children? Insight From Animal Research Models. Policy Insights from the Behavioral and Brain Sciences, 5(1), 126–133. https://doi.org/10.1177/2372732217743990

Schatz Beck, D, & Rostain, A. L. (2006). ADHD With Comorbid Anxiety. Journal of Attention Disorders, 10(2), 141–149. https://doi.org/10.1177/1087054706286698

Smith, K. (2016). 6 Types of Anxiety that Can Affect Children and How to Help. Psycom.net - Mental Health Treatment Resource since 1986. https://www.psycom.net/6-types-anxiety-

and-kids

Talking to Your Child or Teen About Anxiety | Here to Help. (n.d.). Www.heretohelp.bc.ca. https://www.heretohelp. bc.ca/infosheet/talking-to-your-child-or-teen-about-anxiety#:~:text=When%20your%20child%20expresses%20anxiety

Thoma, M. V., La Marca, R., Brönnimann, R., Finkel, L., Ehlert, U., & Nater, U. M. (2013). The Effect of Music on the Human Stress Response. PLoS ONE, 8(8), e70156. https://doi. org/10.1371/journal.pone.0070156

Treatment | Anxiety and Depression Association of America, ADAA. (2019). Adaa.org. https://adaa.org/living-with-anxiety/children/treatment

Types of Developmental Delays in Children. (2019). Nyulangone.org. https://nyulangone.org/conditions/developmental-delays-in-children/types

Walters Wright, L. (2019, October 16). Signs of Anxiety in Young Kids. Understood.org; Understood. https://www.understood. org/en/friends-feelings/managing-feelings/stress-anxiety/signs-your-young-child-might-be-struggling-with-anxiety

What Can Cause a Relapse of Child Anxiety? (2016, February 28). Turnaroundanxiety.com. https://www.turnaroundanxiety. com/hey-boys-im-baaaack-what-to-do-when-anxiety-returns/

Young, K. (2016, May 11). Phobias and Fears in Children - Powerful Strategies To Try. Hey Sigmund. https://www. heysigmund.com/phobias-and-fears-in-children/

Zargarzadeh, M., & Shirazi, M. (2014). The effect of progressive muscle relaxation method on test anxiety in nursing students. Iranian Journal of Nursing and Midwifery Research, 19(6), 607–612. https://www.ncbi.nlm.nih.gov/pmc/articles/PMC4280725/

Katherine Guzman

Made in the USA
Monee, IL
15 June 2023